MORALS AND VALUES IN ANCIENT GREECE

Classical World series
(*Series Editor: Michael Gunningham*)

Athens Under the Tyrants, J.A. Smith
Greek Architecture, R.A. Tomlinson
Greek Tragedy: An Introduction, Marion Baldock
The Julio-Claudian Emperors, Thomas Wiedemann
Morals and Values in Ancient Greece, John Ferguson

Forthcoming
Greece and the Persians, John Sharwood Smith
Aristophanes and his Theatre of the Absurd, Paul Cartledge
A Day in the Life of Ancient Rome, Hilary Deighton
A Day in the Life of Ancient Athens, Hilary Deighton
Ancient Epic: Homer and Virgil, Richard Jenkyns
The Roman Satirists, Michael Coffey
Augustan Rome, Andrew Wallace-Hadrill
Greek Slavery, N.R.E. Fisher
Greek Sculpture of the Fifth Century, J.H. Betts

Classical World series

MORALS AND VALUES IN ANCIENT GREECE

John Ferguson

Bristol Classical Press

General Editor: John H. Betts

First published in 1989 by
Bristol Classical Press, 226 North Street, Bedminster, Bristol BS3 1JD.

British Library Cataloguing in Publication Data

Ferguson, John
    Morals and values in ancient Greece. – (Classical world series)
    1. Greece, ancient period. Morals
    I. Title II. Series
    170'.938

    ISBN 1-85399-118-X

Printed in the United Kingdom by Billings & Sons Ltd.

Contents

Foreword		vii
List of Illustrations		viii
1.	Homeric Values	1
2.	From Shame to Guilt	17
3.	Oligarchy and Democracy	34
4.	Philosophical Ethics	53
5.	The Hellenistic Age	72
Suggestions for Further Study		87
Suggestions for Further Reading		88
Ancient Sources Quoted		96
Glossary of Technical Terms		101

FOR

MICHAEL AND RACHEL

Foreword

I am grateful to the Bristol Classical Press for encouraging me to rethink my ideas on morals and values in ancient Greece some thirty and more years since I first wrote about the subject. This book has a different scope, and a different approach. Besides, Arthur Adkins, to whom I gladly acknowledge my indebtedness, has come in between. I am happy too to share in inaugurating this new series. Inevitably in a short book I have had to omit much of interest. I trust what is left is a fair picture.

Gratitude to the staff of the Press for their skill and courtesy and to Lesley Roff (yet again!) for her indefatigable and indomitable skill at the typewriter (or whatever modern technology has taken its place).

John Ferguson
Selly Park
Birmingham

List of Illustrations

Fig. 1. Odysseus   7
Fig. 2. Odysseus meets Nausicaa   10
Fig. 3. Sappho and Alcaeus   23
Fig. 4. Achilles binding the wounds of Patroclus   39
Fig. 5. The Pnyx at Athens (Mansell Collection)   47
Fig. 6. Socrates (British Museum)   58
Fig. 7. Plato   61
Fig. 8. Aristotle   66
Fig. 9. Demeter   83

Chapter 1
Homeric Values

Minoans and Mycenaeans

A hundred and twenty years ago next to nothing was known about the civilizations of Crete and the Greek mainland during the Bronze Age, especially in the second millennium BC. Excavation has now revealed to us something of these peoples. We call the Cretans Minoans after the legendary king Minos, the mainland Greeks Mycenaeans after the important centre of Mycenae in southern Greece. In Crete Sir Arthur Evans and his successors uncovered for us palaces, carefully built, two or more storeys in height, round a large rectangular courtyard. These palaces were also religious centres, and contained cult-rooms. There was a goddess or goddesses, with the symbol of the double-axe, and male divine subordinates. Bull-leaping was a part of the ritual. So was dancing. The economy was naturally based on agriculture, though there was a powerful fleet and trade with exports of pottery and, probably, cloths and foodstuffs, and luxury imports. We know little for certain about the organization of society. Tradition and the existence of palaces imply kings, probably with councils. We have vivid pictures of the people in frescoes, and also on sealstones and elsewhere. The extreme elegance of the ladies has often been the subject of comment. But our knowledge is of their external appearance only; of the inner life of their minds we know nothing. We do not know what they regarded as good or bad.

Minoan civilization for a time used a pictographic script. Round about 1900 BC this was replaced by a simplified form of writing known as Linear A. This has not yet been deciphered – or rather there have been many rival decipherments, but there is simply not enough material for a persuasive solution. But the brilliant work of the amateur Michael Ventris supported by the professional John Chadwick made it possible to read the bulk of the four thousand or so tablets in its successor, known as Linear B, first found in Crete, but later at Pylos, Mycenae and Thebes in mainland Greece. To the surprise of most, it turned out to be an early form of Greek, using a system of some ninety signs, each representing an open syllable (i.e.

1

a syllable ending in a vowel). At this period Knossos, the greatest of the palaces of northern Crete, had been conquered by the mainlanders, about 1450 BC. The tablets then, which are mainly inventories and accounts, give a picture of the life and structure of the society in the palaces of Pylos in south-west Greece, and Knossos under the Mycenaean Greeks, during some part of the second half of the second millennium BC. We cannot be certain that the same system pertained to other city-centres. It was, as the Greek archaeologist G.E. Mylonas put it, 'an autocratic monarchy with a centralized, bureaucratic administrative system'. There was a supreme *wanax* or overlord, with a deputy or second-in-command, a special class of priests and priestesses, a great many minor officials, artisans carefully classified, and slaves. Some land was held by the *damos*, the whole people. But our knowledge is only of the social and political structure. No literary texts survive, none relating to religious ritual, none even to show what was punishable under the system of justice.

The dangers of translation

Words have a range of meanings when we try to put them into another language – even into another culture or another century. There is a doubtless apocryphal story of a translation of 'The spirit is willing but the flesh is weak' such that the meaning conveyed was 'The liquor is fine but the meat is underdone.' An Englishman in the United States may well be surprised at a notice PAVEMENT NARROWS where he can see that what he himself calls the pavement broadens and the roadway narrows: his pavement is the American sidewalk. An Elizabethan could have prayed without irony 'O Lord if I wish to do that which is right, prevent me; if I wish to do that which is wrong, let me', for to an Elizabethan to prevent was to go in front and clear the way, to let was to hinder (we preserve the sense in a 'let' in tennis).

To a western European, democracy is the right of adult citizens to vote once every few years for the individual or group who will control the political process for the next period; it is likely that a fairly high proportion of candidates will be relatively wealthy. To an eastern European, democracy is a government consisting of people, no matter how they came into positions of power, who profess to have the interests of the working-class at heart; once in those positions they will be relatively privileged. But politicians of both groups tend to use the word 'democracy' emotively, meaning 'those who agree with us'. To an ancient Greek, democracy meant the right of every citizen, adult, male, free and not a foreigner, to participate directly in every state decision, to share in the debate in person (though not many did) and to vote (many did). Payment for attendance at the Assembly meant that there was no occasion to miss out because of loss of income. In addition those who held office were chosen by lot or chance for the most part, and at the end of each year experienced a scrutiny of their term of office and were liable to be indicted before the people's courts. Of course such a system is possible only in relatively small communities, and in a climate where it is predictably possible for large numbers to meet regularly in the open air. None the less no ancient Greek would call the system in Britain or the United States a democracy: he would term it, precisely, an elective oligarchy.

Democracy is a descriptive word meaning 'the power of the commons'; yet there are these immense diversities of meaning. When we come to the words which express value-judgements, good, excellent, just, moral, fine, decent, virtuous and so on, together with their negatives, the borders are even more blurred. If we take the concept of justice alone it brings together a Hebrew word *tsedeq* which is roughly 'righteousness', a Greek word *dikaiosyne*, which is hard to pin down, but seems to come from a root meaning 'way', and the Latin *iustitia* which has to do with the rule of law, modified by the concept of equity, which has the same root as 'equal' and is not far from the idea of fair play. We cannot and must not expect the ancient Greek words to correspond precisely to modern English words. We have to take them on their own terms.

The problem of evidence

There is another general problem we must note.

How can we know what the man-in-the-street thought?

Our evidence is taken mostly from literature. This in itself means that it has considerable limitations:

(a) It is seldom or never written by the man-in-the- street.

(b) It is often written by fairly clever people who have ideas of their own which they want to put over. It is thus unrepresentative.

(c) It may portray an artificial world, of gods and heroes, or shepherds and shepherdesses, for example.

(d) The majority, though not all, of our evidence, especially in the fifth and fourth centuries BC, comes from Athens.

When we look at some of the categories of literature our puzzlement may increase.

(a) The Homeric epics raise questions of how far they reflect the society of the poet's own day, and how far traditions of the past.

(b) Drama raises questions of how far opinions represent those of the character speaking, those of the playwright, or those of his own contemporaries; in tragedy, how far there is an attempt to recreate the heroic past.

(c) The lyric poets are often individualistic and subjective.

(d) Philosophers are attempting a new understanding of the fundamentals of life, and their statements about the views of the man-in-the-street may be misleading.

(e) The orators are liable to overstate, understate or misstate, as it suits their case.

Three important things must be said which point in the other direction.

(a) Literature does provide us with firsthand evidence, to be used with caution no doubt, but contemporary and vital. It is arguable that a novel, a political speech and a poem would give a more accurate picture of the values of the twentieth century than the newspapers with their emphasis on sensationalism (though that itself is an important fact).

(b) Ancient writers (whose work was almost always presented orally and often competitively) had to prove acceptable to the man-in-the-street.

(c) Writers do in fact help to mould the values of the age in which they write.

The Homeric poems

In the long run it was the invention of the alphabet which simplified writing so greatly as to make possible its use for wider usage than inventories and accounts. Eric Havelock has argued that the Phoenicians, to whom the invention is usually attributed, in fact created an abbreviated syllabary at the expense of ambiguity. Thus (to create a simplified example in English) in place of five separate signs representing the syllables BA, BE, BI, BO, BU the Phoenicians used a single sign B, but it might represent any one of five syllabic sounds. So STR might be satire or suture or satyr or siter. The Greeks, by adding vowels to the consonants and using some of the Phoenician consonants as vowels, produced the first true and unambiguous alphabet.

Before the improved possibilities of writing, literature was oral, and its superior memorability meant that poetry developed as an art form before prose. Somewhere about the year 700 BC a bard of genius, living on or near the coast of Asia Minor, created out of the traditional formulaic elements a single epic poem on an episode in the war between Greeks and Trojans, *The Anger of Achilles*. The poem has been called *The Iliad (The Story of Troy)* from the fifth century BC, but it is really a misnomer. The poem was at some point written down, and has been handed on with some accretion and editing, yet still as a single-minded work of art. The poet is named as Homer, and there is no reason to doubt the tradition, or the tradition that he himself was blind, since bards were often blind, and the tradition is early. The ancient world also attributed to him a second epic *The Odyssey (The Story of Odysseus)*, a kind of sequel, certainly composed later, and almost certainly itself composed by a single person, though there are reasons to think that it was not the same person. But we may conveniently speak of the world of the Homeric poems (in the plural).

Both poems deal with legends of the distant past. *The Iliad* in particular hands down bardic traditions from the past. The late Miss Lorimer's great work on *Homer and the Monuments* has shown that there are material elements in *The Iliad* which demonstrably reflect the Bronze Age, in particular the boar's tusk helmet in the tenth book; such objects were not found later; they belong to Mycenaean culture. At the same time the description does not seem to be produced by the poet of the bulk of *The Iliad*. Miss Lorimer has, however, equally affirmed that such elements are less considerable than was at one time supposed, and that the Homeric poems reflect the culture of their own day, and this would be widely accepted.

The social and judicial structures

There is no written code of law: the word *nomos*, the later Greek word corresponding to 'law', does not appear in Homer. Those who give decisions, the king, and elders, are guardians of *dike* (pl. *dikai*), meaning probably 'way', 'custom' and so 'right' but just possibly 'judgement' or 'precedent' and so 'justified claim', and also guardians of *themis* (pl. *themistes*), that which is laid down as established by custom or by previous decisions.

The basic unit of society is the *oikos*, household or family unit, but only in a wide sense more easily grasped in contemporary West Africa than in contemporary Europe. It is within this relation that the idea of *philos*, basically 'one's own', or 'dear' (though without emotional content), operates. There is no real corresponding English word: it implies a mutual relationship involving a tie and a measure of dependence. Our derived words, Philip (lover of horses), philosophy (love of wisdom), philately (love of postage stamps), give no inkling of the basic meaning. But hospitality is an obligation in the Homeric poems, and it can set up a relationship of guest-friendship which extends beyond the immediate or even the wider family. *Xeinos* or *xenos* may mean host or guest, stranger or friend. In this the head of the *oikos* is all important, for this is an aristocratic society.

Socially important is the concept of *time*. The derivation is from *tiein*, to value or honour, but similarity of sound seems to have led to an association with *tinein*, to recompense or pay a penalty. Honour demands recompense. *Time* is the value placed socially on an individual. Each member of an *oikos* has a value set on his or her person or rights, and the head of the *oikos* can demand compensation if these are infringed. This applies to a slave, not in his or her own right, but as a piece of valuable property. It does not apply to foreigners unless they are under the protection of guest-friendship.

Value-words

The primary noun of approval is *arete*, to which we have no corresponding English word, 'excellence' being as near as we can get. The primary adjective is *agathos* (the girl's name Agatha or Agathe is the feminine form), conventionally but misleadingly rendered 'good'. Other near-synonyms are *esthlos* and *chrestos*, the latter having the basic meaning 'useful'.

Arete and *agathos* can hardly be said to denote ethical or moral values at all as we understand them. One of the negative words or opposites, *deilos*, is derived from a root meaning 'fear' – a person who lives his life in fear. It may mean low-born, or simply vile or worthless. The man who is *agathos* – society is at least overtly dominated by males – is the man who is socially effective. In a society frequently engaged in war this implies qualities of courage and leadership, perhaps also of cunning. So those in power are by definition *agathos* and possess *arete*. Their primary excellence consists in birth into a wealthy class, followed by the possession of that wealth by inheritance, a wealth which in Homeric society (before the invention of coinage) consists in land, the products of the land, the animals who take their nourishment from it, the houses and store-rooms built on it, the serfs or slaves operating it.

A group of landowners and their dependents are likely to be knit in a wider community, and there will be certain qualities valuable to that wider community which contribute to *arete* in those who have the primary *arete* of birth and wealth. One such quality in a violent world is that which we usually call 'courage'. The Greeks (*andreia*) and Romans (*virtus*) used words with a root-meaning of 'manliness',

Fig. 1. Odysseus: oinochoe attributed to the Brussels Painter; c. 460 BC.

almost masculine machismo. Something of this toughness was needed to be a successful farmer in relatively unproductive mountain-country, both in the act of farming and in facing dangerous wild animals. Or it might be shown in repelling brigands or pirates: in *The Odyssey* there is a constant assumption that Odysseus and his crew are pirates, and indeed they often behave that way. Or it might be shown in warfare with other communities. Other qualities might contribute to *arete*, some physical, like Achilles's speed of foot, some mental, like Odysseus's cunning or Nestor's gathered wisdom, some intangible, like Agamemnon's leadership even when unwisely exercised. In fact a person who is *agathos* does not lose that quality by behaving arrogantly, unwisely or contrary to the social norm, as Penelope's suitors do in *The Odyssey* by their outrageous behaviour in the palace of the absent Odysseus. Even when their behaviour is subject to the poet's disapproval they are still given the epithet *agathos* or *esthlos*.

This is not to say that there are no words of disapprobation which may be applied to the *agathoi*. There are two, *aischros* (conventionally 'shameful') and *elenches* (something like 'shown up' or 'liable to reproach'). Homeric society is a shame-culture, in the valuable term used by anthropologists, a culture whose sanction is 'what people will say'. The imputation of cowardice is certainly one such. Most pertinently it applies to lack of success, and Odysseus criticizes Agamemnon on these grounds for offending Achilles. He does not suggest that Agamemnon has behaved arrogantly or criminally or ungratefully or lustfully in demanding Achilles's prize woman Briseis, but that without Achilles the Greeks will return home unsuccessful (*Iliad* 2.284-8). The attitude of Thersites is interesting. He is not one of those in power, not an *agathos* but a *kakos*, and is depicted as a radical critic of those in power, and therefore from the point of view of the *agathoi*, which the bard-courtier adopts, a *kakos kakos*. Thersites is himself described as *aischros*, partly because he is ugly, partly because he is cowardly, and partly because he is of bad reputation both with the leaders and with the ordinary soldiers. Yet he criticizes Agamemnon for not recognising Achilles's superior *arete*. In other words the *kakos* accepts the standards of the *agathos*. Gladstone, a sensitive critic, although he did not have the vocabulary of shame-culture, saw that the germinal morality of the Homeric poems lies in the concepts of *aidos* and *nemesis*. *Aidos* is the noun corresponding to *aischros* and means 'a sense of shame'; *nemesis* in its root means the distribution of that which is due and so retribution, the active disapprobation of others. '*Aidos*, Argives' is a kind of battle-cry (Homer, *Iliad* 15.502), 'Argives, show some sense of honour' – almost 'What will people be thinking of you?'

One or two other words are important. *Dikaios* we have touched upon. A person is *dikaios* who follows the norm, the customary way of society. *Dike* is the way things happen and is used in simple statements of fact with no ethical overtones.

> You are like one who, after washing and eating
> Sleeps gently. That is the *dike* of the elderly.
> (HOMER, *Odyssey* 24.254-5)

In *The Iliad*, *themis* is used rather than *dike*: it is connected with 'laying down', and implies rules rather than customs, whether 'laid down' by gods or humans. Another important 'OK word' is *kalos*. This is formally opposed to *aischros*; where *aischros* means 'ugly', *kalos* means 'beautiful'. It is a word of warm, almost emotional approbation, the difference between saying 'X is a good dancer' and 'X is a beautiful dancer'. One other word must be mentioned. This is *saophron*, later *sophron*, and it connotes 'with a safe or sound mind', so 'prudent'.

Women in Homeric society

There is not much in *The Iliad* about the qualities expected of a woman, though there is far more in *The Odyssey*, which sometimes seems to be taking the woman's viewpoint. It is delightful that the queen of the Phaeacians is actually named Arete (*Odyssey* 7.54 etc.). Odysseus may feel *aidos* at being caught naked after a shipwreck, before the princess Nausicaa; she herself has no qualms. The qualities demanded of women are, as Arthur Adkins puts it, 'beauty, skill in weaving and housekeeping, chastity and faithfulness'. The account of Clytemnestra, Agamemnon's wife and murderess, is especially interesting. She is described as *kake*, that is, despite her birth, wealth and success (the ingredients of male *arete*) she has not shown the *arete* of a woman, and she is said to have shed *aischos* on women unborn, whatever good works they might perform (*Odyssey* 11.384, 433-4). Another important passage is the praise of Penelope put into Agamemnon's mouth. She is described as enjoying copious *arete*, and having *agathai* perceptions in her loyalty to her husband Odysseus; in this she is contrasted with Clytemnestra (*Odyssey* 24.192-202). The excellences of the male are inappropriate in the Homeric female.

Fig. 2. Odysseus meets Nausicaa while Athene at the centre looks on; from an Athenian vase of the mid-fifth century BC.

The divine dimension

The Homeric gods are more powerful than human beings: they have greater *arete* (*Iliad* 9.498); they are immortal, whereas humans are mortal. They are not morally better than humans: it has even been suggested that they are morally worse. George Calhoun put it pungently when he wrote in *A Companion to Homer*: 'Punishment for evildoing is scarcely to be expected from gods who themselves commit almost every crime in the calendar. Nor can a pattern of righteous living be sought in the trivial and ignoble character of the Olympians, whose freedom from death and from real suffering keeps their passions engaged on a mean and petty level.'

This is not the whole story. The anger of the gods is aroused by those who use violence to give crooked judgements in the assembly (*Iliad* 16.381-8), those who neglect funeral rites (ibid. 22.358), and, in *The Odyssey*, the conduct of the suitors (*Odyssey* 2.66), or th‿ ₄murder of a guest (ibid. 21.28); they especially protect the rights of hospitality. It will be noticed that these are areas not always easily susceptible of human remedial or retributive action, though it needs to be said that the Homeric Greeks believed that wrongdoers could win the support of the gods by incense, vows, libation and sacrifice (*Iliad* 9.496-501).

There is another major concept, *Moira* or *Aisa*, words which stand for a man's lot or destined portion, perhaps derived from the traditional structural divisions of primitive tribal life, but it becomes personified as Fate, spinning a person's destiny (*Iliad* 20.128). Destiny is sometimes identified with the will of the gods; there is explicit reference to Zeus's *aisa* or dispensation (ibid. 9.608; 17.321). But it is possible to go against one's *moira*.

> Then would the Argives have enjoyed a homecoming beyond their *moira*,
> If Hera had not spoken a word to Athene.
>
> (ibid. 2.155-6)

There is not a total and inevitable determination of human action; but there are limitations within which humans must act and suffer. This is an attempt to wrestle with the age-old questions of freewill and determinism. Poseidon, one of the great gods, tells Idomeneus that anyone who of his own freewill shrinks from the battle is liable to become food for dogs (ibid. 13.231-4). Patroclus, however, is killed by *moira* and Apollo's intervention: the two seem to be equated (ibid. 16.849). There are ambiguities. Zeus banishes the Olympians from the battlefield, picks up a balance, and weighs *kere*, fates of death, of Greeks and Trojans against one another: the Greek side sinks. This is independent of the will of Zeus or any of the other gods (ibid. 8.66-74). Towards the end of the poem Zeus wants to save Hector, but is rebuked by Athene, since Hector is doomed by *aisa* (ibid. 22.178). The point here is that Zeus could go against *aisa* but should not; he will offend against the public opinion of Olympus if he does; he will be liable to reproach. Similarly the common approbatory phrase to a human 'You have spoken in accordance with *moira*' does not refer to an ineluctable destiny, but to appropriate behaviour; it would have been possible to speak otherwise. Occasionally the gods intervene to prevent something happening which would not be in accordance with *moros* (not essentially distinct from *moira*), to prevent Achilles devastating the wall beyond that which is ordained (ibid. 20.30), or Aeneas dying when he is fated to escape (ibid. 20.302).

Of especial interest are some words placed into Zeus's mouth right at the outset of *The Odyssey*.

> Oh, how ready mortals are to put the blame on gods. They
> say that evils come from us when they of their own accord
> In blind folly have troubles beyond *moros*,
> Just as recently beyond *moros* Aegisthus married
> Agamemnon's wedded wife, and killed him on his return...
>
> (*Odyssey* 1.32-6)

Here the action is not governed by an ineluctable destiny. On the contrary: it is freely chosen action outside those bounds.

The person who accepts his destiny is *enaisimos*, which is a term of approbation: he is acting within the limits. Achilles, vaunting over Hector, is not like that: he has gone beyond the limits, he is acting like an animal not a human, he has no *aidos* (which the poet interestingly suggests is sometimes beneficial, sometimes not: the implication is that public opinion is not always right) (*Iliad* 24.40).

Some passages

There then is a general picture of the values which emerge in the Homeric poems. A number of further passages are appended: the reader may like to formulate his own thoughts about them and comments on them. He or she should be able to explain the words in italics. I will then add brief comments at the end.

(a) (Odysseus is addressing Agamemnon about the likely results of his quarrel with Achilles.)

> So I do not direct *nemesis* against the Achaeans
> For being distressed while by their beaked ship. Yet even
> so
> It is *aischron* to wait a long time and return empty.
>
> (*Iliad* 2.296-8)

(b) (Death in battle.)

> His arm fell to the ground covered in blood. His eyes
> Were overpowered by dark death and mighty *moira*.
>
> (ibid. 5.83)

(c) (Hector is addressing Andromache, who is trying to persuade him to stay with her and their child.)

All this concerns me too, wife. But it is terrible
The *aidos* I feel before the Trojans and their long-robed
wives
Were I to behave like a *kakos* and skulk away from the
battle.

(ibid. 6.441-2)

(d) (Hector is addressing Paris, Helen's husband, who is in danger of
being thought a sissy.)

You damned fool, there is no man who is *enaisimos*
Who could pour scorn on your military exploits; you're
stout enough.
But you are shirking and refusing to fight of your own free
will. My head
Is distressed when I hear *aischea* about you
From the Trojans.

(ibid. 6.521-5)

(e) (Ajax is addressing the Greeks when they are on the defensive.)

My friends, be men; set in your hearts *aidos*
Of other humans; each of you recall
Children, wives, possessions, parents,
Whether they be living or dead.
For those not present here I beg you
To stand firm and not turn to flight.

(ibid. 15.661-6)

(f) (Telemachus, son of Penelope and the absent Odysseus, is
addressing the citizens of Ithaca.)

My mother is against her will beset by wooers,
Philoi sons of men who are the most *agathoi* here.

(*Odyssey* 2.50-1)

(g) (Odysseus is ship-wrecked in an unknown country.)

Oh! Oh! What mortals live in the land I've reached?
Are they violent, wild, not *dikaioi*,
Or do they welcome strangers and have god-fearing
thoughts?

(ibid. 6.119-21)

(h) (Odysseus is visiting the land of the dead.)

> This is the *dike* of mortals after death.
> The sinews no longer hold the flesh and bones together.
>
> (ibid. 11.218-9)

(i) (Odysseus has entered his own palace disguised as a beggar.)

> Athene
> Drew close to Laertes's son Odysseus,
> Urging him to go among the suitors collecting crumbs
> To find out which of them were *enaisimoi* and which lacked
> *themis*.
> Even so, she had no intention of saving any of them from
> *kakotes*.
>
> (ibid. 17.360-4)

(j) Telemachus knew long ago that he was in the palace
> But concealed his father's intentions out of *saophrosynai*
> Till he should be avenged on the violence of all too manly
> men.
>
> (ibid. 23.29-31)

Comments

(a) Agamemnon has behaved in a way which is likely to lead to failure. This is reprehensible in him. The speaker does not direct criticism (*nemesis*) against the ordinary Greeks, but if they return empty-handed from a ten-year war they will be *aischroi*, and the objects of public opinion. So through Agamemnon's fault, not their own, they will be objects of shame. Odysseus is not, or not primarily, concerned with the rights and wrongs of Agamemnon's quarrel with Achilles.

(b) Death is the victim's 'share'. The words of themselves do not make clear whether this particular form or moment of death was his inevitable destiny, though later in the poem Aeneas is rescued from Achilles because his moment has not come.

(c) The sanction for his behaviour is public opinion – of the women as well as the men. He uses a simile ('behave like a *kakos*'). There is perhaps a slight ambivalence between 'behave *like* one of the non-*agathoi*, one of the lower classes' and 'show myself a coward' (i.e. be *kakos* while retaining my *agathos*-status).

(d) Any right-minded person can see the courage of the person addressed. *Enaisimos* does not seem a strongly weighted word here, but there is an implication that Paris is not fulfilling his *aisa* or *moira*. He is doing this of his own free will. There is freedom to reject your *moira* within certain limits. In consequence he has the disapprobation of the Trojans. Courage or toughness is treated as a virtue (in our sense) which Paris possesses but is not practising.

(e) This too is a matter of courage. But it is addressed not to the *agathoi* but to the common soldiers. They too have public opinion as their sanction. They must show the qualities expected of a male.

(f) The suitors of Penelope are of noble birth and rich. Their parents are *agathoi*, powerful; so are they. They are *philoi*, objects of natural affection within their own families. Yet they are behaving outrageously. 'Excellence' is a matter of power not of morals.

(g) The approved qualities are to welcome strangers and be *dikaioi* (clearly not just following custom, but the opposite of violent and wild), the disapproved are violence and wildness (lack of civilized society). The sanction is fear of the gods. Personally I find this a very different world from that of *The Iliad*, and cannot think that it comes from the same author or the same age.

(h) Here we have the old meaning of *dike* (for *The Odyssey* certainly does draw on tradition) with no ethical content at all: the way, what happens.

(i) We should not make too much of the goddess, who sometimes seems a piece of epic machinery (though it will not do to eliminate the divine dimension either). There is a moral judgement involved. Some of the suitors are *enaisimoi*. This seems to mean something like the Chinese 'following the *Tao*' – the way of the universe. Others lack *themis*; they do not acknowledge any rules – of gods or humans. And then – she is not going to save either group from *kakotes*. This may mean little more than disaster. But remember that they are *agathoi*: they will be treated as *kakoi*.

(j) Telemachus shows a sound judgement: the italicized abstract is interestingly in the plural. Revenge on the part of a wronged *agathos* is plainly approved. The suitors are *agathoi*. They have courage, masculine prowess: they are *men*. But they are described by an adjective usually translated by the old-fashioned 'overweening' or 'overbearing', but which literally means that they have masculinity in excess. So that we can trace a process which is looking like moral analysis. You can have too much of a good thing, and it needs balancing by other qualities (like having a sound judgement).

Moral values in the Homeric poems

So are there moral values in the Homeric poems?

Of course. There are values of various kinds: some have what we would see as ethical content, some do not. Excellence requires birth, wealth, power, position. To this a male must add courage or manliness. Further, the values are not those associated with Christianity: there is no place for humility, meekness, unselfishness. A woman must add chastity and loyalty; these may not be valued more than beauty; they may be imposed by a male-dominated society; but they are there and they require moral restraint.

The main sanction is public opinion. Fear of the gods is adduced, and the gods are particularly concerned over hospitality: we have noticed that concern is attributed to the gods in areas where offensive behaviour is either not easily detectable or not readily exposed to public reprehension.

But in the concepts of *aisa* and *moira*, *themis* and *dike*, it is possible to discern the idea that the world is an ultimate order, a 'way', which we go against at our peril.

Chapter 2
From Shame to Guilt

Shame-culture and guilt-culture

The anthropologists have taught us to draw a distinction between a shame-culture, broadly one in which the sanction for a person's behaviour is public opinion, and a guilt-culture, where the sanction lies within the person's own conscience, whatever that may be. The distinction is not an absolute one: it was H.L. Mencken who defined conscience as 'the inner voice which warns us that someone may be looking'. In ancient Greece the society of the Homeric poems is, as we have seen, broadly a shame-culture. Across the following centuries there are changes. People do become more introspective. But the attitudes of a shame-culture do not die out: they remain strong for example in Athens during the fifth century BC. A modern example may be used to indicate the complexities. Christian and post-Christian civilization has strong elements of a guilt-culture. But within it in western Europe the youth sub-culture, to take one example, bears all the signs of a shame-culture, and peer-group approbation is a major formative element.

In early Greek society there was a fairly stable land-owning aristocracy. The challenge to this stability came through the development of trade, fostered by the land-hunger which led to the settlement of 'colonies' round the Aegean, into the Propontis and the Black Sea, and on the other side in Sicily and Magna Graecia as far as Cumae and even Massalia (Marseilles). Settlements explicitly designed as trading-posts or *emporia* were rare; rather, the outposts once established, trade with the mother-country might grow by a natural process. Most of the colonies can be dated between 750 and 650 BC, though the movement continued for another century. The effect was twofold. First, it led to closer contacts with foreign cultures, which helped to loosen the ties of the old order. For example, the earliest appearance of the orientalizing style in decorated Greek pottery makes its first appearance about 725 BC in Corinth. Secondly wealth, and so power, no longer depended upon primacy in an established aristocracy based on inherited land. There were new

17

means to power, though no doubt those to establish themselves came from the upper strata of society. This process will have been much enhanced by the invention of coinage in Lydia round about 625 BC. About the beginning of the following century Aegina began to mint its own coinage, followed by Corinth, Athens and other Greek states.

The seventh century saw big political changes, in particular the rise of the first dictators, or tyrants, as the Greeks called them, usurping autocrats, usually from the ruling class. The dictatorships did not last; they seldom went beyond two generations or so; but they upset the ordered pattern of society.

Meantime literacy was spreading. We find whole alphabets painted on pottery, for joy in the achievement. Hesiod's works, like the Homeric poems, survive by reason of literacy. At the same time the greater freedom of expressing oneself in writing combined with social changes to produce a greater individualism of outlook.

Hesiod

Hesiod, from Boeotia in mainland Greece, is thought to have lived at much the same time as the author of *The Iliad*, at a date not far from 700 BC. Two major surviving poems are attributed to him, *Works and Days* and *The Theogony*. There is a slighter poem on *Heracles's Shield*, and we are aware of others which have not survived.

Hesiod is important for two reasons. First, the Homeric poems have their roots in history, even though they may show something of the world the poet knew at first hand. But Hesiod depicts the contemporary scene unmuddied by folk-memories and bardic traditions. Second, Homer, though hardly himself an aristocrat, sees the world from an aristocratic standpoint. Hesiod, though not among the poorer peasants, sees the world from the viewpoint of a peasant farmer, not that of a rich landlord. There are other differences. Homer was by tradition blind, a professional bard. Hesiod was a working farmer. Homer was at home in the relatively sophisticated culture of western Asia Minor. Hesiod had come from the same area (his father was a failed merchant from Cyme) but he settled in Ascra in the backwoods of Boeotia.

Works and Days is overtly directed to the poet's erring brother Perses; it is an attack on dishonesty and idleness, an exaltation of the values of honesty and hard work. There is some feeling that the family may have been *agathoi* but had fallen on bad days, thereby by definition ceasing to be *agathoi* in the old sense; Hesiod says that his father turned to trading out of lack of an *esthlos* livelihood, the livelihood of an *agathos* (634). He is a pessimist about history: in studying the ancient world we need to be constantly reminded that the myth of eternal progress (David Low, the cartoonist, invented two characters Onanonanon and Upanupanup) is comparatively modern, and not plausible to many of today's youth. Hesiod's myth is of degeneration: a golden age followed by a silver age, a bronze age, then for a period a brighter age of 'heroes', and finally Hesiod's own iron age. The interposition of the heroic age is designed partly to do justice to the semi-historical figures of tradition like Heracles, Theseus or Asclepius, partly to blacken his own iron age by contrast. He is critical of the ruling-class, whom he calls 'kings' or 'princes', and urges them to avoid corruption and give honest judgements. They must not behave like the hawk to the nightingale: might is not right. Wealth and power are an essential part of *arete* but not its whole. His sanction is a religious sanction, the anger of the gods. Zeus, the high-god, has 30,000 spirits on duty as a kind of divine police force (252-3), and *Dike* is personified as the virgin daughter of Zeus (256).

But those who are not *agathoi* have standards to uphold.

> You old idiot, Perses, I have *esthla* in mind to tell you.
> *Kakotes* is easily caught, in plenty.
> It's a smooth road; she lives nearby.
> But the immortal gods have set sweat in front
> Of *arete*. It is a long, steep path to her,
> Rough at first too. But when a person reaches the summit,
> Then, hard before, she becomes easy to reach.
> The *best* man of all is one who works everything out himself,
> Noting what is better for his future goal.
> The man who listens to good advice is *esthlos* too.
>
> (286-95)

Here the object is to become rich and powerful. The qualities looked for are means to that end, hard work especially. He says that *arete* attends on riches (312). But not at any price, and Hesiod condemns violence and deceit as a means to wealth, as he condemns wrong done to a suppliant or stranger, adultery in the family, the sexual abuse of orphans, lack of respect for old age (320-34). The ultimate sanction against such behaviour rests with the gods. An interesting passage sets humans apart from other animals.

> The son of Cronos ordained this law for humans:
> Fish, wild animals, birds of the air

> Should eat one another, for *dike* is not with them.
> But he gave *dike* to humans, by far the best
> Of all gifts. Far-seeing Zeus grants prosperity
> To anyone who is willing to proclaim *dikaia* with
> knowledge.
>
> (276-81)

The usage of *dike* has changed. Homer might have said 'This is their *dike*'. But *dike* is now not 'way' or 'custom', but the way of civilized society, the way which maintains the order of society without corruption or bias (Hesiod is conservative not revolutionary), the way ordained by the gods, somewhere within the scope of our 'justice'. Hesiod has put *dike* in the place formerly held by *time*, honour.

Towards the end of *The Theogony* we read of Zeus:

> His second wife was shining Themis, who bore the Seasons,
> Order, Dike, and Peace the flower of them all,
> Who mind over the exploits of humans in their mortality.
>
> (901-3)

Here we see the social qualities Hesiod valued. They are protected by Zeus. They spring from Themis, the personification of 'laying down' as applied to decrees or ordinances. The three great values are *eunomie*, the state of being under good laws or order, *dike*, the customs of a healthy society, free from being led astray by deceit, violence or corruption, and *eirene*, peace. Behaviour directed to these ends is valued; behaviour which endangers such a society – precisely deceit, violence and corruption – is socially and ethically undesirable.

Hesiod is one voice only. But it is unlikely that he was a lone one.

The lyric and elegiac poets

Homer does not appear before us as an individual, except insofar as we can say that *The Iliad* consists of inherited traditions strung together by a single bard to whom we can give a name. But Hesiod is a person in his own right, writing about himself and his family. The poets in the centuries that follow are emphatically not anonymous: they reveal to us their characters and their inmost thoughts, though unfortunately their works survive only in tantalizing fragments.

Archilochus is of uncommon interest. We cannot date him precisely, but must place him in the seventh century BC. He came from the island of Paros. His father was an aristocrat, his mother a slave; he was on the fringes of the *agathoi* but not of their number. He was a soldier of fortune, a gold-digger both literally and metaphorically, an egotist and a genius, who drank and fought and loved and hated. In his verses the anti-heroic note sounds for the first time: he is not ashamed to declare that he threw away his shield in a retreat, finding it an encumbrance. Personal safety is valued higher than the opinion of others; more, there is a pride in not caring about the conventions (Archilochus, *fr.* 6). He attributes all power to the gods, raising the fallen and overthrowing those who have done well (*fr.* 58); success is still valued. But the gods are not central to his thought, and in another passage he attributes everything to *tyche* (chance) and *moira* (man's destined portion or lot) (*fr.* 8). The remedy for trouble in a hostile world is endurance (*fr.* 7), and, in one passage not certainly to be attributed to him, hard work and care for mortality (*fr.* 14). Elsewhere he urges his soul to rise up against seemingly impossible troubles, without exulting in victory or repining in defeat, conscious of the rhythm (probably the ups-and-downs) of human life (*fr.* 57a). He does not appeal to moral probity or religious piety.

The Spartan Tyrtaeus naturally reflects the militarism of the society he knew.

> I would not mention a man or reckon him worth counting
> For *arete* in running or wrestling...
> Not even if he had every glory except might in battle.
> A man is not *agathos* in war
> If he has not stood up to the spectacle of bloody slaughter
> And stood firm reaching out against the enemy.
> This is *arete*. This is the *ariston* of all human prizes,
> And the *kalliston* for a young man to win.
>
> (12.1-14)

But he also says that it is *kalon* for an *agathos* man to die fighting for his country (10.1-2), whereas to suffer want is *aischron* and leads to *kakotes* and lack of *time*. Here we see the old Homeric values, but new values supervening upon them. It is just to say that the hymns of Alcman later in the seventh century give a different picture of Spartan culture and Spartan values. Here we have a religious view, with human life controlled by Destiny (*Aisa*) and Ingenuity (*Poros*), who are described as the oldest of the gods. Fortune (*Tyche*), who becomes increasingly important as the years roll by, is described as daughter of Forethought (*Prometheia*) and sister to Order (*Eunomia*) and

Persuasion (*Peitho*) (64 LP, 52 B, 44 D).[1] Here we have a religious outlook, but by no means a conventional one, and though everything is projected on to the divine scale, there is a strong implication of the sort expressed in a proverb cited by Aesop, 'the gods help those who help themselves'. Destiny and Ingenuity walk side by side. Fortune requires an ordered society, careful planning, and a capacity to persuade others. At first sight to the modern mind there is nothing particularly moral about these values. But when we consider the results of the failure to apply social skills, lack of forethought, social disorder, indifference to persuading others of the best course, we may begin to think the scope of our moral thinking too narrow. But there remains an equation of excellence with success.

The great lyric poets of Lesbos, Sappho and Alcaeus, apart from the magical quality of their verse, are of special interest as depicting two different groups in the same aristocratic society. Male society is composed of bands of 'comrades' ready to fight for their leaders; female society reflects this in its companies for the service of Aphrodite, battling with song and dance rather than swords and spears, but with similarly intense homosexual ties. Alcaeus quotes with approval a saying of Aristodemus to the effect that possessions make a man, and anyone poor cannot be *eslos* (i.e. *esthlos*) or of *time* (360 LP, 49 B, 101 D). Another fragment calls Poverty a *kakon* which cannot be resisted, especially combined with her sister Resource-lessness (364 LP, 92 B, 142 D). Sappho calls Gold a child of Zeus (204 LP) but also says that wealth is dangerous without *arete*, though their combination is the summit of blessedness (148 LP). It is hard to say exactly what she means by *arete*; what is clear is that economic privilege is not enough. Within her own circle she values *philia*, love, friendship, loyalty. Both Alcaeus and Sappho show themselves products of a changing society. Alcaeus, like Archilochus, is not ashamed of confessing to throwing his shield away (Z 105 a LP). Sappho examines herself and frankly reveals the physical and emotional effect on her of the presence of a girl she loves (31 LP).

The verses attributed to Theognis create a major problem of provenance and dating. He himself lived in Megara, and was prominent just after the middle of the sixth century BC. Some of the poems seem to have an earlier point of reference and some a later,

---

[1] This and other similar references show where the original Greek is to be found in the editions of Lobel and Page, Bergk, and Diehl.

Fig. 3. Sappho and Alcaeus, from an Attic kalathos of the early fifth century, by the Brygos Painter.

and lines also appearing in other poets are frequent. They form a block of didactic poetry, mostly attributable to the second half of the sixth century BC, written from the point of view of a disillusioned aristocrat, who is himself confused about the confusion of values, and in particular the changes in the power structure produced by coined money.

> Wealth, mortals have good reason to honour you supremely:
>> You are ready to tolerate their *kakotes*.
> It is the *agathoi* who ought to possess wealth,
>> Poverty is appropriate for a *kakos* man to bear.
>
> (THEOGNIS, 523-6)

Here *kakos* and *kakotes* seem to refer to ignoble birth. This is Theognis's plaint. The *agathoi* have never ruined a city; it is the *kakoi* who introduce violence, corruption and unjust judgements (43-8). He is exercised about interbreeding: the *esthlos* thinks nothing of marrying the *kake* daughter of a *kakos* father, if the dowry is large enough. Wealth has blurred stock: degeneration sets in. The people who used to wear goatskins and did not know *dikai* or laws have suddenly become *agathoi*, and the former *esthloi* are now *deiloi* (53-4). *Dikai* are the ways of civilized society. The powerless have become powerful, the powerful powerless. The values are geared in to social power. But when we read

> Many *kakoi* are rich, many *agathoi* poor
>> Yet we will not exchange
> Our *arete* for wealth, since *arete* is everlasting,
>> But possessions pass from one to another.
>
> (315-8)

arete is not high birth, but a quality of life which is not destroyed by poverty. Theognis does not, and might be hard put to, define exactly what he means. One element he does identify:

> The great glory of *arete* will never die.
> A soldier is the salvation of soil and city.
>
> (867-8)

Courage is the clearest attribute of the *agathos*; we have seen something similar in Tyrtaeus. But other values break through.

> Avoid excess of enthusiasm. The middle way is best of all.
> So,

Cyrnus, you will get *arete*, hard to reach as it is.

(335-6)

Moderation becomes an important factor in Greek ethical thought. Here it appears as means to an end, not as *arete* itself, and *arete* is probably still a position of influence in society, but it is not far from the assertion that moderation is an essential element to *arete* of character. Even more surprising is the quotation

> Be willing to live in piety with few possessions
> Rather than be rich on unjustly gotten goods.
> All *arete* is summed up in *dikaiosyne*,
> Cyrnus: every man is *agathos* if he is *dikaios*.

(145-8)

This is a quite new statement, not that *arete* requires *dikaiosyne* as well as birth and social power, but that *dikaiosyne* constitutes *arete* even without birth and social power.

The Delphic oracle

The oracle at Delphi, associated in Classical times with the god Apollo, and the major oracle of Greece, was the authority on religion and cult-practices, carried considerable weight in politics (especially the settling of colonies), and interested itself in matters of individual morality, which played a relatively small part in early religious practice and were not greatly fostered by the politicians. Delphi for example maintained the principle that purity went beyond ritual to personal attitudes, and responsibility in action went beyond the action to the intention. Herodotus tells a story of one Glaucus, who wanted not to return some money entrusted to him, and asked the oracle whether he should forswear himself to secure the money. He received a stern rebuke and asked the god to pardon him for what he said. The Pythia said to tempt the god and perform the crime were of equal effect. Glaucus returned the money, but none the less his house was extirpated (Herodotus, 6.86). A possibly apocryphal story told how three men were attacked by brigands. One ran away, another in supporting the third accidentally stabbed him, thereby becoming technically blood-guilty. But the oracle refused to have anything to do with the first who would not help his friends, and exonerated the second, declaring him purer than before (Aelian, *Varia Historia* 3.44). This is a remarkable reversal of normal values. Unfortunately we do not know when this story first circulated, though it is likely to have been early, when formal blood-guiltiness was still an issue. A number of stories, which look early, suggest that a poor man who gives regularly what he can afford is more acceptable to the god than a rich man making a large offering (Porphyry, *On Abstinence* 2.15). We have two oracles from a much later period inculcating attitudes of this sort.

> In purity of spirit, stranger, approach the shrine of
> a holy
>   Divinity, after touching the nymphs' spring.
> A tiny drop is enough for the good. A crook
>   All ocean with its streams could not cleanse.
>
> (Greek Anthology, 10.71)

Again:

> The holy places of the gods are open to the good;
> they have no need
>   Of purifications; no stain touches virtue.
> If you are evil of heart, be off. Sprinkling your
>   Body will never wash your soul clean.
>
> (ibid. 10.74)

By the time these were composed *arete* is unequivocally virtue, *agathoi* morally good people. Patterns of thought have changed. But we can see those changes taking place already in the sixth century.

Three maxims were set on the so-called Alcmaeonid temple which replaced the one destroyed by fire in 548-547 BC; the contract was let out to an exiled family from Athens. The maxims are associated with the legendary Seven Sages who were operating in the first half of the century. It is exceedingly unlikely that they dedicated these sayings, but it is probable that the maxims were already associated with the previous temple. The three maxims are 'Know yourself', 'Avoid excess', and 'Go bail and disaster is near.'

An inscription from the front of the temple gives a more comprehensive view of the morality of which the temple officials approved (*Sylloge Inscriptionum Graecarum* 3rd ed. no. 1268).[1]

> Help friends. Control anger. Avoid injustice. Acknowledge religion. Control pleasure. Watch luck. Honour forethought. No oaths. Love friendship. Grasp learning. Pursue repute. Praise virtue. Act justly. Return favours. Cherish friends. Avoid enemies. Cultivate relatives. Shun evil. Be accessible. Guard property. Oblige friends. Hate

---

[1] The Greek text is in this standard collection.

violence. Be gently-spoken. Pity suppliants. Educate sons.
Fulfil your capacity. Be kind to all. Exercise authority
over your wife. Do well by yourself. Be affable. Give timely
answers. Work with a good reputation. Repent mistakes.
Control your eye. Guard friendship. Consider the time. Act
promptly. Dispense justice. Practise harmony. Despise
none. Keep secrets. Respect those in power. Trust time.
Do not indulge in small-talk. Do not glory in your strength.
Accept old age. Use what is beneficial. Speak words of
good omen. Be ashamed of a lie. Shun enmity.

It is somewhat repetitive, conservative, prudential. The old order is
there. It is a world of repute, of friends and enemies. It is an
upper-class morality, involving people in power, and the protection
of property, and accessibility and affability. But there is some inner
self-examination. 'Fulfil your capacity' is something more than
winning others' good opinion; so is 'Be ashamed of a lie', just as the
morality of 'Know yourself' and 'Avoid excess' points to *sophrosyne*.

The cardinal virtues and others

The Christian bishop Ambrose of Milan was the first person to coin
the phrase 'the cardinal virtues' of *sophrosyne, andreia, dikaiosyne* and
sophia or *phronesis*, or in the Latin, *temperantia* ('temperance' or
moderation), *fortitudo* (courage), *iustitia* (justice) and *sapientia* or
prudentia (wisdom). The fourfold scheme is first found for certain in
Plato in the fourth century BC. In *Phaedo, sophrosyne, dikaiosyne* and
andreia are identified, and *phronesis* (wisdom or prudence) added
and set slightly apart (69 C). In *The Republic* (4.427 E, 429 A, 430 D,
432 B, 433 B) he portrays Socrates as seeking the four named virtues
within his political and psychological scheme, *dikaiosyne* ('justice')
being set slightly apart from the rest.

The identification of these several 'virtues' goes back behind
Plato, well into the early fifth century, and probably into the sixth. This
is part of the transformation of *arete* from an excellence which means
primarily social and political power, as we saw in Homeric society, to
an excellence which is primarily or even solely ethical and moral.
Some people have attributed the whole scheme to Pythagoras or the
Pythagoreans of the sixth century, but there is not much to associate
it with the Pythagoreans except the sacredness of the number 4, and
that came to be identified with justice, presumably on the analogy that

2 + 2 = 4 and 2 x 2 = 4 (which was more than an analogy to the Pythagoreans) meaning 'fair shares all round'.

In fact the pattern is by no means fixed or rigid. Well into the fourth century the orators, a fair indication of popular culture, prefer to speak of three great virtues, piety, self-control (*sophrosyne*) and justice (Isocrates, *On the Peace* 63) or courage, justice and self-control (Demosthenes, *On the Crown* 215). Xenophon lists the qualities which Socrates is anxious to define, as piety (*eusebeia*), followed by justice, wisdom, goodness (*to agathon*), nobility (*to kalon*) and courage, without mentioning *sophrosyne*. Piety is in fact quite as important as the others. The dramatist Aeschylus in the first half of the fifth century BC can single out the '*sophron, dikaios, agathos, eusebes* 'man' (*Seven Against Thebes* 610) naming self-control and justice, and along with them goodness (whatever that means) and piety. There is some tendency to link 'virtues' with different stages of life, and courage is particularly associated with early manhood, and wisdom or piety with old age. But it will not do to overschematize this, though there may have been popular saws to that effect. There is an important passage in Pindar celebrating a victory in all-in wrestling probably in 475 BC.

> At the test a goal
> Is revealed of the things in which one may excel others,
> A boy among boys, a man among men, or thirdly
> Among elders, according to the several portions possessed
> By us mortals. Four *aretai* are brought
> By mortal life, bidding us face the present with prudence.
> (*Nemeans* 3.70-6)

This has sometimes been taken as early evidence for the four cardinal virtues and their association with different stages of life. In fact the passage says nothing of the kind. It says that excellence is shown in different ways at different stages of life, naming three stages. It does not say that the excellences are moral, though there is an implication that a certain moral fibre (*andreia?*) is requisite at all three stages when it comes to the test, and that we should at all stages face life with *phronesis* (prudence) – which is therefore not the peculiar virtue of the elderly. But the passage is difficult, and we may sympathize with the German scholar who said that the longer he considered it the more obscure he found it.

We can thus see that if we except the more general words *arete,*
agathon and *kalon* there are some six ideas which dominate the ethical
thinking of the Greeks from the sixth century. *Sophia* and *phronesis*
are best kept separate. *Sophia* is not far from our 'wisdom'. *Phronesis*
(Latin *prudentia*) is more like practical good sense: its absence leads
to disaster (Democritus. *frr.* 102; 191). The Delphic precept 'Know
yourself' is an aspect of it. 'Avoid excess' is an aspect of *sophrosyne.*
This, as we have seen, has no precise English equivalent: the several
renderings 'self- control', 'moderation', 'temperance', 'obedience' are
none false but all too limited. *Saophron* is the opposite of *oloophron*
'with destructive thoughts' and some later Greeks took it as meaning
'with saving thoughts' (Aristotle, *Nicomachean Ethics* 6.1140 b 11;
Plutarch, *On Tranquillity* 470 D). It has often been called the typical
Greek virtue. Surely not: they talked about it because they too seldom
possessed it. *Andreia,* courage or manliness, is straightforward
enough. It was a quality expected of the Homeric soldier, and the later
Greeks had wars enough in all conscience, though *andreia* could be
shown in other situations (Aristotle, *Rhetoric* 1.9.8.1366 b).
Dikaiosyne is harder: we have seen Theognis saying that it comprised
all *arete* (147); the same aphorism is found in Phocylides, a
contemporary of Theognis, who came from Miletus in Asia Minor (*fr.*
14). It is the principle of right behaviour in social relationships. On
top of all these is *eusebeia* or *hosiotes.* They are not quite the same,
though related. *Eusebeia* is not far from the Latin *pietas*, but wider
than our piety. It is the observance of a sacred duty towards the gods,
members of the family, or friends. Its opposite may be opposed to
dikaiosyne (Aeschylus, *Seven Against Thebes* 598). But the sense of a
religious obligation is primary (Theognis 1141-4; Pindar, *Olympians*
3.41-8.8; Aeschylus, *The Libation-Bearers* 122), and in *hosiotes* is
always there. With this concept *arete* is linked to religious observance.

Pindar

Pindar (518-438 BC) is important because, though literature has to be
used cautiously as a guide to life, his choral lyrics reflect the values of
his aristocratic patrons. To Pindar *arete* (I avoid complicating matters
by using his dialectal form) means both excellence and the success
which follows upon it. Thus Pelops and Hippodameia produced six
sons who were eager in *aretais* (plural) (*Olympians* 1.89). As those six
included Atreus and Thyestes with their record of fraternal

quarrelling, seduction, adultery, deceit, murder and cannibalism they are hardly being held up as moral examples. Yet we may read that

> *aretai* without danger
> Win no honour among men or in hollow
> Ships.
>
> (*Olympians* 6.9-11)

(It will be noticed that public opinion is still a criterion.) Again 'The kindly *arete* of Croesus does not fade away' (*Pythians* 1.94). Here the meaning is excellence, and in the last passage there is an element of moral approval. But equally a man may win *arete* by athletic prowess (*Olympians* 7.89; *Nemeans* 5.52); here the meaning is success won by excellence.

Four factors are needed for *arete* in Pindar's view. The first is *phya*, breeding. This is the old aristocratic requisite of high birth, though somewhat extended. The second is wealth (*Olympians* 5.15; *Isthmians* 1.42; 5.10). The third is effort, which is coupled with the outlay of wealth in the three passages cited. The fourth is the favour of the gods, and without that there is no success. If two men equal in breeding, wealth and effort compete, the one who wins possesses, the one who loses lacks, the favour of the gods.

> That which comes from breeding is in every case best.
> Many men
> Have striven to win glory
> By *aretai* gained from training.
> Without God anything
> Is not worse for remaining unsung.
>
> (*Olympians* 9.100-4)

It is glory, fame that Pindar extols:

> Creatures of a day! What is a man? What is he not? A man
> is
> A dream of a shadow. But when a gleam comes as a gift
> from the gods
> A bright light and a kindly life rest on men.
>
> (*Pythians* 8.95-7)

Some passages

We will look at some further passages; again the reader may like to think out their implications.

(a)   Then from the widewayed earth to Olympus,
        With their noble bodies wrapped in white robes,

Forsaking humankind for the company of the immortals,
Aidos and *Nemesis* will go. Bitter griefs will be left
For mortal men. There will be no help against evil.

(HESIOD, *Works and Days* 197-201)

(b)   How long are you going to lie down? When will you have a
stout heart,
        Young men? Are you not ashamed, before your neighbours,
Of all this indolence? Do you intend to sit in peace
        When the whole land is full of war?

(CALLINUS *fr.* 1 (c. 650 BC))

(c)   Be firm in your mind. Always let gentleness rule your tongue.
        A quick temper is a sign of the lower classes.

(THEOGNIS, 365-6)

(d)   Concentrate on *arete*. Set your heart on things *dikaios*
        Do not let gain conquer you when it is *aischros*.

(THEOGNIS, 465-6)

(e)   Wealth adorned with *aretai* gives the opportunity
For this and that. It holds a profound care for a quest.
It is a conspicuous star, a true light
For a man. But if, possessing wealth, he knows the future,
That wicked spirits of the dead promptly here
Pay the penalty, that sins committed in this realm of Zeus
Are judged in the underworld by one who pronounces
The account with inescapable sternness.
But with nights and days
Always alike, enjoying the sun, the good
Receive a life less troubled.

(PINDAR, *Olympians* 2.54-63)

(f)   A man has great power by inborn glory.
The man who has only what he has learned, is living in
darkness, inconsistent,
Never coming down with firm tread, sampling myriad *aretai*,
with incomplete purpose.

(PINDAR, Nemean 3.36-55)

Comments

(a) Hesiod, though not an aristocrat, is deeply imbued with Homeric values. *Aidos*, shame, fear of the censure of others, and *Nemesis*, the consequences of that censure, are here personified. In his view they are the only restrictions on anti-social behaviour. The consequence of their loss would be evil, social disaster.

(b) Callinus, an obviously militant poet from Ephesus, is challenging the young aristocrats to leave their banquets and go into battle. Except that it is a present situation rather than an epic of the past, the sentiment is very Homeric. The qualities valued are energy and courage (seen as a single attitude).

(c) Theognis is class-conscious. This is almost an example of *noblesse oblige*. Two qualities are praised – firmness of mind, an aspect of *phronesis*, and control of tongue and temper, an aspect of *sophrosyne*. But is his censor external or internal – the opinion of others, or a man's self-opinion? At the least it is becoming ambiguous.

(d) *Arete* here has a moral element. But society is no longer controlled by land-owners. This is a situation where wealth, however achieved, brings power. Theognis is deterring people from pursuing gain by anti-social means. In another passage (147-8) he says that all *arete* is summed up in *dikaiosyne*. Wealth without observance of the social rules will not bring *arete*. Here he sets *dikaios* against *aischros*, a word suggesting that the sanction is public opinion, but moving towards a shame which is inwardly felt.

(e) This difficult passage is of considerable importance. Power ('the opportunity for this and that') is not called *arete*, but consists in wealth adorned with *aretai*. Pindar does not here refer to birth or breeding, prominent in other parts of his poetry. But *aretai* are not 'virtues' but excellences of different kinds, such as the things which bring victory in the Games. The reference to the 'quest' is obscure. It implies that the man of *arete* is continually searching (for glory?).But then Pindar goes on to quote as sanction not public opinion in this life, but punishment after death, in the underworld or in an inferior reincarnation ('here'): the passage is important for Pindar's religious views, and the nature of the religious sanction (in Homer it might be, for certain offences, the angry intervention of the gods during the offender's lifetime). And here the qualities demanded are ethical, without which wealth, even adorned by *aretai*, will not save him.

(f) A simple statement of Pindar's belief in breeding as necessary to a man for him to be *agathos*. Training is not enough. *Aretai* here are not in our sense virtues, but excellences of various kinds.

Chapter 3
Oligarchy and Democracy

The City-state

The geography of mainland Greece divides much of the country into quite small coastal plains ringed by mountains. Each of these would have numbers of farmsteads and villages and a central town and market, with a hill or acropolis, which combined the attributes of a fortress with a sacred place because near the sky where the gods lived. The town was often a little way from the sea as a precaution against pirate-raids. A *polis* or city-state, the political unit of classical Greece, consisted of this township and the countryside round about. A small island might constitute a single *polis*; on a larger island there might be two or three. The city-states were of very various sizes and populations. Attica, the area with Athens as its city, comprises about 2500 square kms and had a total population in the middle of the fifth century BC of perhaps a quarter of a million or slightly more; Syracuse in Sicily was 4700 square kms with a comparable population. The island of Delos was under 5 square kms.

Citizens with political power were a limited proportion of the whole population. As in all states at all times there was an age qualification. As always until less than a century ago, women were excluded. Resident aliens did not have citizen rights unless these were specially granted to individuals. These included slaves. Some states incorporated a subject people in their neighbourhood who had a measure of self-government but not citizenship of the *polis*. There were property-classes, which might be used to restrict citizenship to the wealthy. Citizens might be deprived of citizenship for wrongful behaviour.

Although the Greeks were divided amongst themselves in this way, and frequently at war, they were proud of their Greekness, and contrasted their standing as Hellenes or Greeks with the *barbaroi* ('barbarians' who made unintelligible noises like 'bar-bar-bar'). The quadrennial festival at Olympia (the Olympic Games) was a time of truce: otherwise the only impulse to unity was the threat from Persia, and when that threat from time to time appeared, it was not more than partial.

Political changes

The old kings, found in the Homeric poems, had largely given way to a Council of upper-class elders. In some places the office survived, in the far north on the fringes of the Greek world, or in Sparta where we find two kings balancing one another, five ephors (annually elected) with a great deal of power, a Council of twenty-eight elders, and an Assembly of limited function with hardly more than 4000 members in all. In Athens, and some other states, the title of 'king' remained attached to one of a group of state officers conveniently called 'magistrates' or archons. The rule of a powerful minority is usually called oligarchy (the rule of the few) or aristocracy (the power of the 'best' – but we have seen that the 'best' means those who have power). In such orders the commons or *demos* had little or no say. But we have noted at the beginning of the last chapter how in the sixth century a disaffected noble sometimes staged a coup as an unconstitutional monarch, a dictator or 'tyrant'. Many of these 'tyrants' were not unenlightened: at Athens Pisistratus did a great deal to turn the city into a major cultural centre (see *Athens under the Tyrants*, also in this series). Each must have had some kind of loose party behind him, without which he could not have survived; sometimes they appealed to the commons. The effect of a couple of generations of dictatorship was to weaken the hold of the old aristocracy, though they frequently reasserted themselves in and after the expulsion of a dictator.

Democracy, the power of the commons, perhaps goes back to the assembly of the armed forces in time of war. There was always a threat to the power of the upper classes in the very numbers of the commons should they become disaffected, as they had plenty of cause to be, and this is why the dictators found them useful allies. Anything like full democracy was not achieved until the very end of the sixth century BC, and really not till the middle of the fifth. Athens was the most influential democracy. All power was in the hands of the Assembly where all citizens might attend, speak and vote; decisions were taken by majority vote. Payment for attendance removed the economic barrier. Most offices of state were held for one year, and the holders chosen by lot – chance. The exceptions were a few priests, whose office might be hereditary or subject to different conditions, some finance-officers, and the generals, who were commanders in war and expected to give a lead in the Assembly, and who were elected annually, normally from the ranks of the old aristocracy. All officials were subject to scrutiny at the end of their term of office, and trial for mismanagement before the people's court with a jury too large to be bribed. The Council of 500, which prepared Assembly business, was chosen annually by lot, and served in committees of 50 for one-tenth of the year each; the chairmanship rotated so that each citizen had a chance of being President of the *polis*, as it were, for one day.

Stasis, political disturbance between different factions, often those supporting oligarchy and democracy, was all too common and all too bitter. It is important to note that the class-structure with a property-qualification meant in a sense that democracy was an extended oligarchy, and oligarchy a limited democracy. It was relatively easy, though politically traumatic, to move from one to the other by granting to or removing from the lowest property-group or groups the full political rights of citizenship.

Solon

Solon was prominent in Athenian politics in the early sixth century BC (For a fuller discussion of Solon, see, *Athens under the Tyrants*, also in this series). Later generations were liable to see him as the founder of Athenian democracy, but he was in fact a moderate oligarch. His primary reform was to cancel debts for which land or liberty of person was the security, redeeming peasants sold into slavery, and restoring peasant-farms. He put a permanent end to serfdom or slavery for debt. At the same time he encouraged trade and industry. He established a clear class-structure on an economic basis, defined the political powers of the Assembly, and instituted the Council. He did not end poverty, and he did not introduce democracy, though he made its introduction possible.

Solon was a poet as well as statesman and has left an incomparable record of his achievement and attitudes. The first thing we become aware of is that he is a *moralist*, and a religious moralist. He believes that everything is under the control of the Destiny (*aisa*) of Zeus and the blessed immortal gods (4.1-2). He believes in a class-society, divided simply between the aristocracy (*esthloi* or *agathoi*) and the commons (*demos*). When he uses the word *kakoi* in opposition to *agathoi* or *esthloi*, it is hard to say whether he is thinking purely of the social structures and means the lower classes, or whether there is an ethical dimension and he is referring to those of the lower classes who break the bounds of *dike* to challenge the social order. 'Many *kakoi* are wealthy, many *agathoi* are poor' (15.1). Again 'I did not approve that the *kakoi* should have an equal share in the fat of the fatherland with the *esthloi*' (34.8-9). He is puzzled by the power of wealth, which disrupted the social order, but he has no answer except the plea for moderation. He is old-fashioned in many ways: he appeals to *aischos*, shame or dishonour, as a sanction (3.2). *Dike*, to which he constantly appeals, is for him something like the order of society. He praises *eunomia*, the state of having and observing good laws, and condemns *dysnomia*, the state of having bad laws and not observing the laws.

> This is what my heart bids me teach the Athenians,
>   That *dysnomia* brings a city many evils,
> That *eunomia* makes everything orderly and fit,
>   And often puts fetters on the *adikoi*.
>
> (4.31-4)

Fetters are not a punishment, but a control, a limitation on action. Order in society meant so much to him that we find him saying 'Obey the lawful authorities whether their commands are *dikaios* or *adikos*' (41). That is a paradox, but it shows the ambiguities of concept at the time. It remains a major political and social issue today how a citizen should behave in face of unjust laws. Later, at the beginning of the fourth century, Socrates in Plato's *Crito* says that he accepted the protection of the laws when they were in his favour and he could not conscientiously evade their verdict when they went against him. But that, because personal, is not the whole story, and there is always the question whether the disruption of society is greater through the existence of an unjust law, or the breaking of law to challenge it, and indeed of a conscientious refusal of unjust commands. Solon was a conservative who knew when it was politic to give way. 'I granted the commons just enough rights to suffice' (5.1). He claimed to stand with a strong shield embracing both parties (5.5); his legislation was protecting them. He saw society as disrupted by folly (the opposite of *sophia* or *phronesis*), by allowing the pursuit of wealth to take precedence over everything else, by *adikia* of purpose, by *hybris* (a difficult word which conveys arrogance of attitude with violence of action, including rape and bodily damage, and is sometimes opposed to *sophrosyne*), and excess, especially but not solely on the part of the leaders of the commons (4.5-10).

Solon divides human life into ten periods of seven years each. He characterizes the first three in purely physical terms. The fourth is marked by strength as a sign of *arete*. The fifth is the time for marriage and the production of children. The sixth is a period of mental training and an elimination of antisocial ambitions. The seventh and eighth are the periods of excellence in mind and tongue. These are still strong in the ninth, but his tongue and *sophia* are less firm in leading to the height of *arete*. If he survives to the end of the tenth it is time to meet his destiny (*moira*) of death (27). It will be noticed that *arete* means excellence generally and the respect of his fellows, and that it is achieved at different stages by physical strength, the generation of children, the control of antisocial tendencies, eloquence and wisdom. It will also be noticed that Solon is not interested in the *arete* of women, and that his men are scarcely expected to reach 70, and certainly not to live beyond that.

Friendship

Solon in one passage (13.5) prayed to the gods to be sweet to his friends and bitter to his enemies. This attitude long persisted. In Plato's dialogue, Meno actually defines *arete* as the capacity to help friends and harm enemies (Plato, *Meno* 71 E).

We have noted in the Homeric poems (p. 6) that *philotes* (later *philia*) represents a tie, usually reciprocated (though it can apply to things as well as people); even in the Trojan War Diomedes has a closer tie to the Trojan Glaucus by reason of the guest-friendship of their grandfathers, than to a Greek who is not so bound to him though on the same side in the war (Homer, *Iliad* 6.119-236). So *philotes* or *philia* is, in Adkins's phrase, 'the basic structure of co-operative life'. One of the classic friendships of myth was that between the Athenian hero Theseus and the Lapith Pirithous, which seems to have begun when Theseus caught Pirithous raiding Marathon. They entered into a compact, and were thereafter bound to one another's support, as in the kidnapping of Helen and the attempt to kidnap Persephone. The Greek words thus represent a more formal and less emotional tie than our 'friend' and 'friendship', which we will now use as the best English words available. It will be noticed that it is an exclusive concept applying to a limited circle.

Friendship thus is a social value in itself, but in the sixth and fifth centuries it comes to be the subject of a number of qualifying aphorisms, attributed to the gathered wisdom of one or other of the

Fig. 4. Achilles binding the wounds of Patroclus; from interior of wine-cup by the Sosias Painter, c. 500 BC. The close friendship of these heroes determines much of the action of The Iliad.

Seven Sages. 'Do not make friends quickly, but when you have made them, be sure to keep them.' 'Treat your friends as if you will one day hate them, for most men are bad.' 'It is better to have one good friend than many bad ones' (here the terms are ethical). 'One ought to benefit a friend so as to increase his friendship, and to transform an enemy into a friend.' 'Be the same to friends in prosperity and adversity.' 'Be more ready to share in your friends' adversity than in their prosperity' (Diogenes Laertius, 1.60,87, 105,91, 98,70). It is for the most part prudential and not very profound.

In the Pythagorean communities of Sicily and South Italy we find emerging a number of epigrammatic precepts which expressed the internal and practical solidarity of the 'school'. Four are particularly relevant, and, though it is notoriously difficult to be certain what in Pythagorean traditions is early and what is late, these seem likely to be early. They are 'One soul', 'The things of friends are held in common', 'Friendship is equality', and 'A friend is a second self.' The first and fourth are close to one another, and express an identity of purpose and experience between those who have accepted the common discipline of the community. The second and third show a practical consequence in the sharing of goods and possessions. This did actually happen, but there is some indication that an arithmetical equality gave way to a geometrical equality of proportion and that (to adapt George Orwell) some animals became more equal than others.

There was some speculation about the basis for friendship in nature. A Homeric tag 'God always draws like to like' (Homer, *Odyssey* 17.218) was used to defend the view that 'Birds of a feather flock together' (in the modern expression) and that the root of friendship lies in likeness of outlook. This might be linked to theories of sense-perception, that in smell the air outside meets air of similar density within the brain or that there must be a fire in the eye to account for the perception of light. Much later, this attitude leads to the theological proposition 'Unless you make yourself equal to God, you cannot apprehend God, for like is known by like' (*Corpus Hermeticum* 11.20). The other view is that sense-perception takes place by contrasts, and friends should complement one another.

The Pythagoreans were involved in politics, and the ties of friendship were politically significant. The word used tends to be *hetairos*, originally comrade-in-arms or messmate, though *philos* is also found. The clubs may have originated as religious associations and their attraction in the mid-fifth century may have been intellectual and social companionship, but in the latter part of the century they increasingly became in Athens upper-class political enclaves opposed to the democracy, and it was in them that the oligarchic revolutions were planned. The restored democracy banned such political associations, but they returned as social fellowships.

One additional point. Classical Greek knew literally thousands of words compounded with *syn*, representing togetherness. In Homer there are not more than fifty, and the verbal forms almost always refer to an action of gathering a group together. But from the lyric period a new group of words comes into being, when the collectivity refers to the subject not object, and the verbs refer to the inner life of mind and spirit: a typical example is the original from which we draw our word 'sympathy'. There is thus an emphasis on communal action moving towards an emphasis on communal attitudes leading to action. There is the need, within the group, for togetherness, almost regardless of the nature or object of that togetherness. In the second half of the fifth century a few voices are raised challenging this. Sophocles puts into the mouth of his Antigone 'My nature is togetherness in love not hatred' (Sophocles, *Antigone* 523), Euripides into the mouth of Jocasta 'It is a bitter thing, togetherness with the unwise in unwisdom' (Euripides, *The Phoenician Women* 394).

Homonoia

A particular political value which the Greeks stressed is *homonoia*. It means literally 'like-mindedness', but 'unity of purpose' expresses it better. *Philia* tended to be limited in extent; within a single *polis* different groups of *philoi* might be daggers drawn. The result was *stasis*, civil disturbance, whose course in Corcyra Thucydides dissected with clinical analysis (3.80-4). Isocrates, towards the end of a long life, summed it up with bourgeois intensity: '*stasis*, murder, unmerited exile, confiscation, maltreatment of women and children, revolution, debt cancellation, redistribution of land and other intolerable disasters' (*Panathenaicus* 259). *Homonoia* was the answer to this. 'You would all agree', said Lysias, 'that *homonoia* is the greatest blessing a state can have, and *stasis* is the origin of all our troubles' (18.17).

Antiphon wrote a treatise on *homonoia* in the second part of the fifth century, but it is not wholly clear which fragmentary snippets are excerpted from that work, other than a few isolated words. He did say in the treatise that new friendships are close, but not as close as old ones. A passage, not certainly from the same work, holds up anarchy as the worst possible state for mankind, and goes on to argue for the discipline of children so that they may be disciplined adults. There are certainly political implications there, and a suggestion of conservative attitudes.

Gorgias, sophist and teacher of rhetoric (c. 485-375 BC), made a celebrated speech at Olympia on the subject of *homonoia*. Unfortunately we do not know the exact date of this. 408 has been suggested, but it may be later. Equally we know little about it. It was, however, an advocacy of *homonoia* not just within the individual state, but among all Greeks: the Olympic Games was an appropriate occasion for such a plea. We know that he saw the qualities of courage and wisdom as necessary to that end. Further, an anecdote tells how he was pilloried for advocating *homonoia* among the Greeks when he could not achieve it between himself, his wife and maid. It is reminiscent of the (true) story of a British peace leader of the 1930s who had a cook and housemaid at loggerheads. His wife said to him 'E——, this can't go on. We've a peace meeting in the drawing-room and war in the kitchen.' It is reminiscent too of a parable used by a slightly later Greek, Python (or Leon) of Byzantium, in the middle of the fourth century. 'Gentlemen', he said, 'you see my build. But I've actually got a wife much fatter than I am. When we're of one mind, any old bed does for us. If we quarrel, the whole house isn't big enough.' (Athenaeus, 12.550 F; *Suda* sv Leon).

Isocrates (436-338) was the natural successor to Gorgias, who taught him. Curiously, his lack of confidence and the weakness of his voice, meant that he, a consummate rhetorician and teacher of rhetoricians, made more impact through the written word than through the spoken. Modern judgements of him have gone from extreme to extreme. Some have seen in him a far-sighted statesman, others a petty politician. He regarded *homonoia* as essential to the happy state together with political security, economic prosperity, and a good reputation (*On the Peace* 19); the last is of particular interest as it shows the persistence of the values of the shame-society. In a monarchy it was the function of the ruler to foster *homonoia* (*Nicocles* 41). But, like Gorgias, Isocrates advocated *homonoia* between the states of Greece, and suggested that war between them should be regarded as no less disastrous than internal stasis (*Panegyricus* 174). He saw that unity was more easily achieved in opposition to something than in pursuit of a common end, and, much as the USA and USSR sank their differences in facing Nazi Germany, pleaded with the Greek states to sink their differences in facing Persia (*Panegyricus* 3). When they showed no signs of doing so freely he looked to a champion, such as Philip of Macedon, to bring them together auto-cratically. In the end something of the sort happened.

Homonoia was an important political value towards which some Greeks began to aspire.

Physis and nomos

One of the most important debates with political implications was that between *physis* and *nomos*. *Physis*, literally 'the way a thing grows', comes to mean 'nature', though sometimes it is helpful to think of it as 'reality'. *Nomos*, originally 'the way a thing is apportioned', and then 'something that is believed in or practised as right', may mean 'a law' and it may also mean 'something that is artificial or conventional'. This antithesis of itself leads to ethical debate. Humankind may be said 'naturally' to behave in certain ways. Law or social convention limits the area of permitted behaviour. Is this an unwarrantable imposition on personal freedom, or the fact that raises humans above wild animals and makes them civilized?

It is not clear exactly when or by whom the debate was inaugurated. Aristotle (*Sophistical Refutations* 173 a 7) calls it a widely recognized stock question. Archelaus, a fifth-century natural philosopher who is said to have influenced Socrates, offers probably the earliest example. This was much the time when philosophers held that judgements of sweet and bitter, hot and cold were subjective: these qualities exist by *nomos* not *physis*.

This, as indicated already, does not necessarily involve a rejection of these conventions. It is a commonplace of the second part of the fifth century that they produce civilization. The chorus in Sophocles' *Antigone* affirm that technology is morally neutral, but to honour the *nomoi* of one's country and the *dike* of the gods exalts a *polis*. Protagoras, the greatest of the sophists, in Plato's dialogue puts forward a myth that *dike* (a sense of justice) and *aidos* (a sense of shame, with the censor moving from external opinion to internal conscience) were not innate in humans from the first, but that Zeus had to send Hermes to bring these qualities without which political unity and stability are impossible; further, that they had to be implanted in measure in every human (Plato, *Protagoras* 322 A-323 C). Protagoras calls these civic or political *arete*, and contrasts it with other *aretai*, such as excellence in music. Protagoras was an avowed agnostic in matters of religion: the myth represents the results of historical experience. Similarly an anonymous late fifth-century writer, a conservative of no great profundity of thought, whose work has been recognized in the works of the much later philosopher Iamblichus, argues that if humans merely followed *physis* life for everyone would be nasty, brutish and short. Certainly excellence depends on natural endowment, but on natural gifts subjected to *nomos*, which forms a particular bulwark against dictatorship. (In Diels-Kranz *Fragmente der Vorsokratiker* 89).[1] Again, the orators, a sure index of stock views, echo similar thoughts. One example will

---

[1] This German work, referred to hereafter as DK, is the standard collection of the Greek fragments of the so-called Presocratic (really Preplatonic) philosophers. The actual quotations are translated in K. Freeman *Ancilla to the Pre-Socratic Philosophers*, Oxford: Basil Blackwell, 1948.

suffice. A passage in a speech *Against Aristogeiton*, which may or may not be by Demosthenes, declares that in every city men are governed by *physis* and *nomoi*. Nature is disorderly and varies with the individual; it may be anti-social and lead to depraved acts. The *nomoi* are shared, ordered and the same for all and commend justice (*dikaion*), the good (*kalon* here) and the advantageous. Without the *nomoi* there is licence; it is obedience to *nomoi* that raises humans above the animals (25.15-6).

Immoralists tend to exalt *physis* above *nomos*. The otherwise unknown Callicles in Plato's *Gorgias* is the most eloquent exponent of this view. He has no time for those who profess to educate the youth in *arete* (520 A). *Nomoi*, covering both law and convention, are established by the majority to do down the strong. To Callicles better, more powerful and stronger are synonymous (488 B-D); that is, in nature there are no moral sanctions. Nature reveals the fact that it is just for the better man to have more than the inferior, and the more able than the less able (483 D). A similar view is found in an important papyrus fragment of Antiphon from his work *On Truth*. He states that laws and conventions impose an artificial standard, and that justice consists in not transgressing these. His advice about the best way of handling this situation is to observe the laws in the presence of witnesses, and when alone to follow the precepts of nature (DK 87 *fr.* 44). Again, Critias in his satyr-play *Sisyphus* makes Sisyphus say that at one time there was no punishment for *kakoi*, no reward for *esthloi* (it will be noted that the words are wholly ethical here). Then humans invented laws. Open crimes of violence were prevented. Covert crime continued. Then some brilliantly ingenious man invented the idea of gods who punish even secret acts, so veiling the truth in lies.

Another view found is to treat *nomoi* as a kind of superior *physis*, or at least to say that there is a superior *nomos* ordained by the gods. Heraclitus, about 500 BC, had said that all human laws are nourished by one divine law (DK *fr.* 114). A good later example is found in Demosthenes's most eloquent speech when he says of the punishment of crime, but not of error 'This will be found not only in the actual laws but nature has personally decreed it in the unwritten laws and in human hearts' (*On the Crown* 275). Aristotle calls unwritten laws universal and according to nature (*Rhetoric* 1368 b 7, 1373 b 6, 1375 a 32). Sometimes the moralists, like the immoralists, say that the *nomoi* do not exist by nature, and they must follow the unwritten laws which

are ultimately the nature of things. So in the exchange in Sophocles'
Antigone:

> CREON: You had the effrontery to break the laws?
> ANTIGONE Yes, for it was not Zeus who proclaimed them,
>   Or Dike, enthroned with the gods below,
>   Who enacted laws of this sort for humans.
>   I did not think that your edicts had the power
>   To override the unwritten, unchangeable
>   Laws of the gods – you are mortal.
>   Those laws are not of today or yesterday:
>   They live for ever and none knows their origin.
>   (449-57)

The oligarchic slogans

The oligarchs, old aristocrats and *nouveaux riches* for the most part,
had two great slogans. One was *eunomia*, a condition of good laws.
Hesiod (*Theogony* 901 ff.) had associated *Eunomia* with *Dike* and
Eirene (Peace). Solon had proclaimed the very thing at Athens.
Alcman at Sparta spoke of *Prometheia* (Forethought) as mother of
Tyche (Fortune), *Eunomia*, and *Peitho* (Persuasion). Sparta with its
rigid, unchanging conservatism was a model for the Athenian
oligarchs; it came to be contrasted with the Athenian democracy's
espousal of *isonomia*, equality under the law. The oligarchs also
played on the ambiguity of *agathoi* as the aristocracy and the
meritorious, to claim that in democracy the *kakoi*, the undeserving,
usurped the function and place of the worthy. So in the debate in
Herodotus between the Persian nobles (who are asking whether
monarchy, oligarchy or democracy is preferable), which reflects a
debate in fifth-century Athens, Megabyzus advocates oligarchy
simply because it is the rule of the *aristoi* (the ambiguous 'best') and
the best people will produce the best policies (3.81). The author of
the right-wing pamphlet *The Constitution of Athens* begins from the
objection that the constitution of Athens puts the interests of the mob
above those of respectable people. For the rest the pamphlet is an
attack on the practice of Athens, the permissive attitude to the
behaviour of slaves, the exploitation of the rich, the imperialism, the
refusal to be bound by alliances and agreements. The upper classes,
he says, are honourable, trustworthy and consistent.

The democratic slogans

The two great democratic slogans were freedom and equality. Freedom includes freedom of action (*eleutheria*) and freedom of speech (*parrhesia*). So Shelley – addressing Liberty, found his mind turning to Athens:

> For thou wert and thine all-creative skill
> Peopled with forms that mock the eternal dead
> In marble immortality that hill
> Which was thine earliest home and latest oracle.

Plato in the fourth century caricatured the ideal of Athenian democracy. The city is full of freedom and frankness; everyone does what he wants, goes to work or stays at home; the city becomes a jumble-sale; and the mind becomes a democracy, a popular assembly of impulses and fancies with majority voting and the noisiest getting the floor.

The great word for equality is *isonomia*, equality before the law. The idea first appears in a drinking-song, ironically produced in some upper-class circle, celebrating the assassination of Hipparchus:

> I'll bear my sword in a myrtle-branch,
> Like Harmodius and Aristogeiton,
> When they killed the dictator
> And made Athens equal before the law.

But the oligarchs espoused the idea only in opposition to a dictator, and the historian Thucydides records *isonomia* as the political programme of the mass democracy (3.82.8; 4.78.3; 6.38.5). The interesting fact is that the advocates of democracy stress law as well as equality. So in the Funeral Speech Pericles says that the Athenians do not copy the laws of their neighbours, but practise democracy, and their laws allow all to take part in equality (*ison*). They are kept from doing wrong by respect for the laws (Thucydides, 2.37). An interesting passage comes in Euripides' tragedy *The Suppliant Women*. A herald from Thebes arrives in Athens and asks peremptorily 'Who is dictator here?' (399). Theseus, a constitutional monarch, answers, in defiance of chronology, that Athens is free, and that the poor have equal rights with the rich (403-9). Dictators are menaces. They allow no common laws: one man keeps the law to himself, and that is not *ison*. When the *nomoi* are written down the powerless and the rich have an equal *dike*. The lesser with justice on his side can defeat the great. Freedom means that anyone with a good policy can propose it, and win renown

Fig. 5. The Pnyx at Athens, the hill near the Acropolis where the Athenian democratic Assembly met.

for it, and keep silent if he has nothing useful to propose. What could be more *ison* politically? (429-41)

The Funeral Speech

The Funeral Speech attributed to Pericles by Thucydides is often taken as the supreme evocation of Athenian democracy (Thucydides, 2.35-46). It was delivered over the bodies of the dead during a bitter war. It is patriotic, even imperialistic. It starts from the ancestors, in justice to them and appropriately to the occasion. Then the speaker breaks into the defence of democracy we have already glanced at. He stresses the freedom of their political life directed to the common weal, and the freedom accorded to eccentric private behaviour, and goes on to speak of the city's rich cultural life. The Athenians do not take immense precautions over military security, because they rely not on secretive preparations but on their own good spirits, and they do not spend long periods in military training in their youth. One out of many famous passages follows:

> We do not become extravagant in the pursuit of beauty or soft in the pursuit of wisdom. Wealth is for us an opportunity for acting rather than a subject for boasting. To admit to poverty brings no disgrace, but disgrace is attached to a failure to take practical steps to escape from it. Our citizens are involved alike in private and public activities; close involvement in your own affairs is not incompatible with being politically well-informed. We are the only people who regard the man who takes no interest in politics as useless rather than harmless. We personally decide or have a proper debate on public issues. We do not think that words get in the way of actions. What is disastrous is to enter into an action without working out the consequences beforehand. We show a rare combination of qualities, a capacity for adventurous action and for deliberation about our undertakings. Other people's bravery is ignorance: reflection breaks hesitation. Spiritual power comes from a clear knowledge and just evaluation of what lies ahead, danger and glory alike and going forward undeterred...In a word, I affirm that our city is an education to Greece.
>
> (THUCYDIDES, 2.40-1)

The speech, idolized and idealized in the past, has come in for rough handling by some recent critics as a hymn of complacent self-worship (covered by a mask of moderation and by soporific rhetoric) which ignores injustices and treats as facts ideals only partially realized. This is of course true. A politician is no more on oath than the composer of lapidary inscriptions. But the Funeral Speech shows us the values which the Athenian democracy took as their ideals and liked to think that they possessed.

Some passages

(a)   I long to possess wealth, but have no desire to get it
            Unjustly: *Dike* always follows.
       Riches given by the gods come to a man
            Firm from bottom to top.
       Riches which men chase with violence, do not come
            In proper order, but induced by unjust actions.
       They follow reluctant. Ruin quickly joins them.
                                                    (SOLON, 13.7-13)

(b)   I fitted straight *dike* to each individual
       And wrote ordinances treating *kakos* and *agathos*
       Identically.
                                                    (SOLON, 36.18-20)

(c)   Join us Greeks together
       Again from the start
       With the elixir of *philia*.
                                        (ARISTOPHANES, *Peace* 996-8)

(d)   *Homonoia* is generally agreed to be the greatest blessing a
       state can have. Governing councils and leading citizens
       regularly tell the people to achieve *homonoia*. Everywhere in
       Greece there exists a law that the people must swear to practise
       homonoia: everywhere they take this oath. I do not believe the
       purpose of this is merely to ensure that they vote for the same
       dramatic companies, approve the same musicians, exalt the
       same writers, and have the same tastes; it is to ensure that they
       obey the laws. It is where the people uphold the laws that a
       state achieves strength and prosperity. But without *homonoia*
       no state and indeed no family could be in a healthy condition.
                        (Socrates in XENOPHON, *Memorabilia* 4.4.16)

(e)   ION: I must have a word
       With Phoebus. What's up with him? Raping girls
       And abandoning them! Producing children in secret
       And leaving them to die. Just stop it! You're mighty:
       Pursue *aretai*. Whenever a mortal shows
       A *kakos* nature, the gods punish him.
       How is it *dikaion* for you gods to write laws
       For mortals, and lay yourselves open to a charge of
       lawlessness?

                                    (EURIPIDES, *Ion* 436-43)

(f)   Someone will say that a democracy is not sagacious and not
       ison either, and that those who have property are also better
       at ruling best. But I say first that democracy is a name for all,
       oligarchy for a part only. Secondly the wealthy are best at
       looking after property; the sagacious offer the best policies; the
       majority, after hearing the debate, are the best judges. Further,
       these classes severally and conjointly have identically an equal
       share in a democracy. An oligarchy gives the majority of the
       people a share in the dangers, but claims a larger share of the
       benefits – indeed grabs them all and keeps them. This is what
       the powerful among you with some people avid for change are
       set on – you cannot hold that course in a great city.

                              (Athenagoras, a populist politician in Syracuse
                                            in THUCYDIDES, 6.39)

Comments

(a) Solon, a moderate oligarch, who opened the door to
democratic changes, in this passage reveals something of his personal
beliefs. Wealth is a key to power, but he will not acquire it antisocially
– for fear of divine punishment. Dike is almost equivalent to the part
played earlier by Nemesis. The worst antisocial behaviour is *hybris*,
violence. This is a disruption not just of the social but of the cosmic
order. It is noticeable that Solon upholds the class structure based on
wealth, but also seeks a moral basis for society. The moral order is
divinely ordained (the personification of Riches as reluctantly
acceding to the crook is entertaining). The sanction is fear of
punishment and disaster.

(b) Here Solon justifies his political and social reforms. *Dike*
here (not personified) is the established practice of society,

established in this instance by legislation. It is straight because it is clear and unambiguous, of immediate application and fair. There is an irony in a claim to fit *dike* to each individual, and to say the *kakos* and *agathos* receive identical treatment, but Solon wants each individual to feel that his claims have been recognized. *Kakos* and *agathos* are here 'lower-class' and 'upper-class'. There are here the seeds of the later democratic watchword of *isonomia*.

(c) Aristophanes produced the comic drama *Peace* in 421 BC in the hope of peace after nearly ten years of war between Athens and Sparta. Here *philia* is seen as the condition of peace. *Philia*, originally a tie primarily affecting individual heads of households, took on wider political implications, but still tended to apply to groups within the state. Aristophanes uses it not even of a cement within a whole *polis*, but extends it to unity among all Greeks. Something similar happened to *homonoia* (unity of purpose) in the mouth of Gorgias and his followers.

(d) A clear exposition of the political value of *homonoia* (unity of outlook or unity of purpose) within a single political community. There are a few interesting overtones in the passages. 'Governing councils and leading citizens' implies oligarchy, but equally Socrates (rightly) says that cultivation of this value of *homonoia* is universal among the Greeks; even dictators, having got rid of opponents, would pay lip-service to it. Socrates links *homonoia* with obedience to the laws: this, though with different emphasis, was a slogan of oligarchs and democrats. The state's pursuit of strength and prosperity makes one think that the state is viewed as a kind of aristocrat. Socrates recognizes in effect that the family is the simplest form of social unit; Aristotle is to make the same point at the outset of his *Politics*.

(e) A fascinating passage. Ion, a somewhat priggish young attendant at Apollo's temple at Delphi, has learned of a rape committed by his god and master. The boy's reactions are delightfully characterized. There are two main points of interest in terms of moral values. First, the gods are seen unequivocally as the source and decreers of human morality, and do not even observe their own decrees. Admittedly Ion is a character in a play, in religious service and pietistic, but the view must have been widespread. Second, the language, which used not to be ethical but descriptive of social role, and then became ambiguous, is now purely ethical – *aretai* is 'virtues', *kakos* is 'wicked', *dikaion* is 'just'.

(f) It is interesting to set this defence of democracy alongside that of Pericles in the Funeral Speech. One value is introduced, which we have not exactly encountered elsewhere, sagacity (*synesis*). It is not far from *phronesis*, practical wisdom. Athenagoras does not find it in property-owners (oligarchs did claim it for themselves). Nor does he claim it for the commons. He claims that the commons will decide best between the recommendations of the sagacious. He does not explain the oligarchs' suggestion that democracy is not *ison* (the complaint was more often that democracy imposed equality on unequals) but he answers it fairly enough with a bitter jibe at the practice of the oligarchs. The words 'those who have property are better at ruling best' lays on thick the claims of the upper-classes and the ambiguities of good, better and best. His special claim for democracy is that it involves everyone.

Chapter 4
Philosophical Ethics

The early philosophers

It would not be at all true to say that the early philosophers were not interested in questions of how human beings ought to live, though our records tend to be dominated by questions of natural philosophy and cosmology.

Xenophanes of Colophon may have been born around 570 BC and lived well into the next century. Later Greeks saw him as the founder of the Eleatic school of thought, and teacher of Parmenides, possibly. That he was a moralist can be seen in his attack on the gods of Homer and Hesiod.

> Homer and Hesiod have laid at the feet of gods
> Everything that humans find a reproach and shame,
> Theft, adultery and mutual deceit.
>
> (DK21 *fr.* 11)

He assailed anthropomorphism, noting that Negroes have black, snubnosed gods, Thracians red-headed and blue-eyed gods, and that if cattle had gods they would be in the shape of cattle; he believed in one ultimate, not to be conceived in human form. He noted the relativity of sweet and sour, and so paved the way for an ethical relativism which he probably did not himself hold.

His successor Parmenides, like Xenophanes, wrote in verse, and paradoxically denied time and plurality, affirming that the only statement legitimately to be made is 'That which is is.' But the myth which prefaces his philosophical exploration, giving it the force of a religious revelation, exalts Truth, and Dike, who is personified, represented as an avenger and coupled with *themis*. It is hard to know exactly what Parmenides means by *dike*. It is not the custom of humans. It might be loosely rendered justice, but is not to do with human law or ethics as normally understood. It is more like the Tao, the Way of Things.

It is extremely hard to say what is early and what is not in Pythagoreanism. Dualism appears in the Table of Opposites (Aristotle, *Metaphysics* 1.986a 23-7).

Limit	and Unlimited
Odd	and Even
One	and Many
Right	and Left
Male	and Female
Rest	and Motion
Straight	and Curving
Light	and Darkness
Good	and Bad
Square	and Oblong

Good (*agathon*) and bad (*kakon*) are not ethical terms here, but they are terms of approbation and disapprobation. We also find it said that *arete*, excellence, is a proper fitting together (*harmonia*), like health, all good, and God (Diogenes Laertius, 8.33). On a rather different level are a string of popular and even magical precepts, to which at some point allegorical interpretations were added. Thus 'Don't stir the fire with a knife' means 'Don't stir up passion or pride'; 'Don't step over the beam of a balance' means 'Don't overstep equity and justice'; 'Don't sit down on a bushel-measure' means 'Take equal thought for today and tomorrow'; 'Don't eat your heart out' means 'Don't let your life waste away in troubles and pains'; 'Don't turn round when going abroad' means 'Don't cling on to life or be magnetized by its pleasures when departing from life' (Diogenes Laertius, 8.17-8). Some of these rationalizations were in circulation during the fifth century BC. Beyond this we have noted a stress on friendship and community: this seems to have incorporated men and women equally. The doctrine of reincarnation may imply a pattern of divine reward and punishment.

Heraclitus of Ephesus, who was active around the year 500 BC, was notoriously obscure and aphoristic. He claimed that there was one single wisdom, understanding the way in which the universe is directed (DK22 *fr.* 41). This one wisdom 'does and does not agree to be called by the name of Zeus' (*fr* 32): this implies that it is ultimate, but not a personal God. We can get no impression of an ethical system. 'A dry soul is wisest and best' (*fr.* 118): Heraclitus thought that fire is the basis of the material world. 'All human laws are nourished from one single divine law' (*fr.* 114), 'A human being's character is his *daimon'* (*fr.* 119) – perhaps his guardian, perhaps his destiny. Beyond that we cannot discern much except for a dislike of excess.

Empedocles came from Acragas in Sicily and was active about the middle of the fifth century BC. He held a complex cosmogony by which there were four 'roots', earth, air, fire and water, and two controlling forces, love (*philia*) and strife. Strife aims at a state where all four are separate, love at a single homogeneous unity in which all four are mingled. A world like ours can arise only during an intermediate period in the cosmic cycle, and Empedocles, a pessimist, said that in our world strife is dominant. In relation to humans he wrote of a state of primal innocence. The primal sin was bloodshed, alike of animals and humans. Like Pythagoras, Empedocles believed in reincarnation, and he seems to have regarded 'prophets, hymnodists, doctors and princes' as the highest earthly incarnation, after which comes immortality (DK31 *frr.* 146-7).

But, apart from the fact that respect for strangers is included among good deeds (*fr.* 112), we cannot trace an ethical code which might win a higher life.

The sophists

There were fifty years of relative peace and prosperity in mainland Greece between the Persian Wars and the Great War between Athens and Sparta. Growing members of the upper classes found themselves with time on their hands. A group of able teachers filled a gap by offering classes for a fee in a wide variety of subjects; they were themselves peripatetic. These were the 'sophists'; the word originally meant 'expert'.

It was an age of widening horizons, scientific curiosity and increasing scepticism of established values. Hecataeus of Miletus wrote *Journey Round the World*, in which he described different life-styles from Spain to India. The historian Herodotus of Halicarnassus recounts with some gusto a story of how Darius brought together a tribe of Indians who ate their dead parents, and some Greeks who cremated theirs: each was scandalized at the other's practice (3.38). Herodotus does not judge; custom rules. Similar relativities are spelt out at length in a sophistic work from the end of the century called *Twofold Arguments* (*Pros and Cons* is a better title). For example the Peloponnesian war was both good and bad, good for the victorious Spartans, bad for the defeated Athenians. The Macedonians think it honourable for girls to have sexual experience before marriage, the Greeks count it shameful. The whole thing was put on a more scientific basis by the Hippocratic doctors, practitioners of clinical science, based on the island of Cos, and founded in the fifth century by Hippocrates. *Airs, Waters and Places* stresses the fact that geographical environment affects physique and mental capacity and attitude. All of which is a part of the debate between *nomos* and *physis*.

The sophists professed to teach *sophia* (wisdom). Aristotle said that they taught the semblance not the substance of wisdom (*Sophistical Refutations* 165 a); Socrates, according to Xenophon (*Memorabilia* 1.6.13), called them prostitutes for offering wisdom in exchange for money. Or they might claim to teach *arete*. The word is still ambiguous, and in the hands of some practitioners it meant 'how to get on in society'. This in itself was ethically amoral, and could become ethically immoral. To make the worse cause appear the better is a constant aim of politicians and lawyers, and Athens and other states were highly litigious and political; but it easily moved from strengthening the presentation of a weak case to gilding an immoral course with a superficial coating of morality. With the sophists this was complicated by the fact that though many of the leading teachers were men of the highest integrity, they tended to an overt agnosticism. Protagoras of Abdera, most distinguished of them all, expressed agnosticism in religion, claimed that there were two sides to everything (Diogenes Laertius, 9.51), and, in a famous and still puzzling aphorism, said 'Man [or 'A human being'] is the measure of all things, of the existence of the existent and the non-existence of the non-existent' (DK80 *fr.* 1). This may be a denial of any divine basis for value-judgements. But it may mean that each individual is arbiter of his or her own truth. What seems sweet to me is sweet; if you say 'No', that sweetness is non-existent – for you. It is a small step to go further. What seems just to me is just; if you say 'No', that justice is non-existent – for you. There is no objective criterion.

The typically sophistic position (in a hostile view) is expressed by Thrasymachus in the first book of Plato's *Republic*. It must remain doubtful whether the picture is a fair one, as one of the few certainly authentic fragments of Thrasymachus (DK85, *fr.* 8) says 'The gods do not oversee human affairs. They would never have neglected justice, the greatest of human goods. As it is, we can see that human beings never use it.' In Plato, Thrasymachus argues that justice (*dikaiosyne*) is simply that which is in the interest of the stronger party. Justice is obedience to law; the laws are made by the stronger party in their own interest; so justice is that which is in the interest of the stronger party. Thrasymachus is not sufficiently thoroughgoing an immoralist to sustain his paradox. The two especially interesting matters are the popular view which relates a quality which has a strongly ethical element to observance of the laws, and the sophistic assumption that it is all subjective anyway.

One value the sophists unanimously agreed on is education. But education is a means not an end.

Socrates

With Socrates we face a major problem. It is not appropriate here to go in detail into the so-called Socratic Problem. It is enough to say that we have two principal sources for our knowledge of Socrates (there is a late life by Diogenes Laertius, and a caricature in Aristophanes *The Clouds*). One is Xenophon, in whose pages he appears a pietistic, prosy moralist. The other is Plato, in whose greatest dialogues he is shown as a brilliant constructive metaphysician. Neither can be authentic. If (as we must) we accept the evidence of Aristotle, Plato has put his own metaphysical constructs into his master's mouth. But if Plato has imposed his own, very different genius on Socrates, Xenophon has created a Socrates equally in his own duller image. The Athenians would never have executed Xenophon's Socrates. The view taken here is that the picture offered in Plato's early dialogues is broadly authentic. To this we should add that incidental references in fifth- and fourth-century literature show that his contemporaries regarded him as a politically subversive sophist.

Aristotle adds his evidence that Socrates busied himself with ethical topics (*Metaphysics* 1.987 b 1). Xenophon (whose evidence may be confidently accepted when it accords with that of others) says:

> He was always discoursing about human matters, considering what is piety, what is impiety, what is *kalon*, what is *aischron*, what is *dikaion*, what is *adikon*, what is *sophrosyne*, what is madness, what is courage, what is cowardice, what is a city-state, what is a statesman, what is authority over human beings, what does it mean for a person to possess it...
>
> (*Memorabilia*, 1.1.16)

Fig. 6. Socrates.

What the authentic Socrates does not seem to have done is to provide answers to his questions. For example, in Plato's *Laches*, after a discussion of a display of fighting in armour, Socrates comes round to asking what is *arete*; he then isolates the part of *arete* which fighting in armour is supposed to promote, courage (*andreia*). What is courage? Laches, a soldier, says that it is not running away in battle. Socrates has no difficulty in showing that there is a courage shown in retreat. Laches now moves from giving an example to a definition of a sort: courage is a kind of endurance of the soul. This will not do: for foolish endurance is not a quality to be admired – and yet is it not more courageous to endure against the odds than with them? Nicias, another soldier, joins in, and after some sparring, proposes that courage is a knowledge of things to be dreaded and dared. Socrates leads him to admit that this involves a comprehensive knowledge of past, present and future, good and evil – far wider than courage. The dialogue ends in *aporia*, helplessness. So in the first book of *The Republic* various definitions of *dikaiosyne* (justice, right conduct) are essayed and rejected: telling the truth and restoring anything deposited with us, helping friends and harming enemies, the interest of the stronger.

The evidence of both Xenophon and Plato shows that Socrates thought of excellence, *arete*, in terms of function, and used analogy from craftsmanship and other skills. There is a particularly good example towards the end of the first book of *The Republic* (352 B-4 A): the *arete* of a pruning-knife is to prune, of an eye to see, of an ear to hear. This involves a teleological view of the universe, and, as Xenophon presents it, an anthropocentric view, by which the natural world serves the needs and pleasures of humans. The question inevitably follows: in what does the *arete* of a human being consist? Socrates gave the answer that it lay in the care of the *psyche*, conventionally 'soul', but including under a single head the life-principle, the intellect and the moral personality. *Arete* does not come from possessions (as in the old order), though possessions may follow upon *arete*. Socrates's conception of *arete* is thus ethical, yet wider than ethical.

Socrates was famous for two paradoxes. The first asserted '*Arete* is knowledge'. This is a deliberate paradox, not a definition. It includes self-knowledge; it includes a knowledge of the goal, the aim, the *telos*, which means that it includes a commitment to action; it includes a total knowledge of the circumstances. If a person does that which is wrong or bad, do they really *know* what they are doing? Hence the second paradox 'No one does wrong willingly'; if they do wrong, they do so either in ignorance or under duress. To do wrong always harms the doer: no one willingly harms themselves. Here analogy is important, and Socrates uses an analogy between wrongdoing and disease.

Socrates claimed not to teach. Born to a sculptor and a midwife he claimed to follow not his father's profession but his mother's. He did not press another person into a mould of his own devising: he enabled them to give birth to the thoughts that were in them. That the claim was authentic is shown by the variety of philosophical positions held by his associates. His questions were often leading questions, but it is not possible to build a system out of his words.

Democritus

Democritus of Abdera is usually treated as a Presocratic, but he was younger than Socrates, and lived to a great age. The contribution to atomic theory, for which he was famed, was published in 405 BC. The ethical maxims attributed to him are also given to one Democrates, probably but not quite certainly a misspelling of his name; they belong to the fourth century. Democritus was a hedonist, who found the goal of human life in happiness, for which he uses a variety of terms. It is a property of the soul (DK68, *fr.* 170). Sometimes he speaks of wellbeing, or cheerfulness, or freedom from disturbance (*ataraxia*). When he comes to the means to this end he tends to a negative view, and recommends avoidance of excess (*fr.* 233); excess destroys enjoyment. Other things to be avoided include silly hopes (fr. 292), envy (fr. 191), greed (*fr.* 219), miserliness (*fr* 227), bellicosity (*fr.* 237), pleasure in others' misfortunes (*fr.* 289). Among positive qualities he singles out courage (*fr.* 213) as a help in facing calamities, justice *(dike: fr.* 215) and wisdom (*fr.* 216), but does not elaborate on them.

Plato

We come now to the two great systematic thinkers, Plato and Aristotle. It is impossible to do more than touch upon some of the main tenets of their thought.

Plato (427-347 BC) had been influenced by Socrates when he was young and Socrates old. He records Socrates's inconclusive search for values, not content with popular sayings or particular instances,

Fig. 7. Plato.

seeking to know what it is that courageous acts (say) have in common
which makes them all courageous, yet never finding the answer. He
studied with the followers of two earlier thinkers, Parmenides who
said that true reality cannot change, and Heraclitus (and his follower
Cratylus, with whom Plato studied) who said that the world around
us is for ever changing. Then he went to South Italy and Sicily, met
the Pythagoreans there and absorbed their mathematical philosophy.
A geometrical proposition, such as Pythagoras's theorem, that in a
right-angled triangle the square on the hypotenuse is equal to the sum
of the squares on the other two sides, is, on the face of it, a permanent

truth. Yet it is never more than approximately true of a triangle drawn in the sand with a pointer. It is true, not of the triangle we perceive with our eyes, but of the triangle we apprehend with our mind. Plato found here a key to unlock all doors. For we have never seen a perfectly courageous action, we have never seen absolute beauty (*kalon*). So Plato devised his Theory of Forms. True reality belongs to an unchanging world of forms, the form of beauty, the form of courage and the like, apprehended only with the mind. Things in our material world are always imperfect, always changing, fleeting. Everything comes to an end: what is lasting? Only the forms, said Plato. Things on earth imitate, or participate in, the eternal forms, but always imperfectly. Beyond the world of forms lies the form of the good (*agathon*), the ultimate in Plato's mature philosophy. Good is not ethical, or not merely ethical. It must lie beyond the forms, because the forms must be good. Plato mystically adds that as the sun produces in eyes the capacity to see and in material objects the capacity to be seen, so the form of the good produces in minds the capacity to know and in the forms the capacity to be known.

Plato's *Republic* is a search for *dikaiosyne* (justice, right behaviour). To facilitate the search Plato passes from the individual to the community: the assumption that what will be found in one will be found in the other is important. Starting from a basic and not at all ideal community, and moving from there to a fevered, frantic, expansive military imperialism he unexpectedly passes to a discussion of the best organization for a city-state, and opts for a relatively small, highly qualified ruling class, without access to money (corruption) or family (nepotism), and with none of the normal perquisites of high office. The rest, rich and poor, traders and business men, farmers and artisans, form in political terms a lower class. The ruling class is subdivided between the 'Guardians' proper, and the Auxiliaries, who have the potential but do not quite make the grade, and who form the fighting forces and administrative support. Plato similarly divides the *psyche* into three. There is reason at the top, and desire at the bottom, and in between a quality he calls temper, or mettle, or 'the spirited', which sides now with one part, now the other. A personal example may help. As a schoolboy I was running home to play cricket when I saw an old lady with a heavy burden walking in the other direction. Reason told me to help her with her burden; desire told me to get to cricket. Desire won, and for fifty years I have been saying to myself 'What a rotter you were not to help that poor old lady!' But had I followed reason my spirited element might well have been saying 'What a quixotic fool you were!' It will be noticed that the parallel is not perfect: in the macrocosm the upper class is subdivided. Indeed in *Phaedrus* Plato depicts the tripartite soul as a chariot in which a charioteer (reason) tries to control two horses, one white and spirited, one black and decidedly unruly: there it is the lower division which is subdivided. Plato assigns the *arete* of wisdom (*sophia*) to his upper class and to reason, courage to the second class and to the spirited element. Logically we expect him to say that *sophrosyne* (self-control) belongs to the lower class and to desire. For some reason he does not do so: he treats it instead as a kind of fitting together or harmonious concord of all sections. This in fact somewhat detracts from the effectiveness of his identification of *dikaiosyne* with a situation where wisdom rules, courage acts in accordance with the dictates of wisdom, and *sophrosyne* allows no internal conflicts, whether in the individual or in the state. *Dikaiosyne* effectively becomes a restatement and reinforcement of what he has already said. At the very end of *The Republic* Plato justifies *dikaiosyne* in a myth of reward and punishment after death.

We shall look at one other dialogue by Plato, *Philebus*, written late in his life. The theme is pleasure. Plato had discussed it before, in *Gorgias* with puritanical hostility opposing pleasure-seeking to the pursuit of good, and with greater subtlety in *Protagoras*. The discussion in *The Republic* relates pleasure to the Theory of Forms, recognizes intellectual pleasures as the purest, because free from pain, while allowing a place for the lower pleasures provided they remain under the authority of reason. *Philebus* starts from a discussion whether pleasure, joy and delight and all that goes with them are good for all living creatures. But pleasure is a complex concept, and neither pleasure nor wisdom alone can be the supreme good. The good life must contain a balance of knowledge and pleasure. The world in which we live comes from the impression of Limit or Measure on the Unlimited or Indeterminate by an agent or first cause. Mind is related to cause, pleasure belongs to the unlimited; yet pleasure as we know it is in the mixed class of being. There follows a complex analysis. First, pleasures are divided into those of the body and those of the *psyche*: but the division is not absolute, for all consciousness involves the *psyche* and bodily pleasures may permeate through to the *psyche*. A second division involves pleasures of anticipation, which patently may be true or false. A third division relates to intensity of pleasure. Finally there is the division between pure pleasures and those mixed with pain. The highest are the pure pleasures, above all the contemplation of beauty (*kalon*) and truth. But pleasure, changeable as it is, cannot be the good, which is constant, unchanging and absolute. For humans, the good life will include pleasure and knowledge. But in the ultimate scale of goods the top place is held by things which display order and measure, the second that which is beautiful or noble (*kalon*) and symmetrical, the third intellect and wisdom because they partake of truth, the fourth particular areas of scientific and practical knowledge, with pleasures in the fifth place, and then only pure pleasures. It will be noted that the examination in *Philebus* is individual not social.

Lodge (see 'Further Reading') listed a number of candidates for Plato's highest good: 1. Pleasure (which has its place, but not the highest). 2. Wealth (contributory only). 3. Health (a consequence of the good life). 4. Power (not the goal but a movement towards it). 5. Happiness (coincident with the ethically ideal life). 6. The life of the ideal statesman (this would offer the circumstances for the best life, but is not available). 7. Immortality (to the Greeks equivalent to divinity). 8. Goodness of character (the four *aretai* of *The Republic*). 9. *Sophrosyne* (an aspect of this). 10. *Dikaiosyne* (similar). 11. Genius (certainly an aspect). 12. Religion (only as philosophically reformed). 13. Science (an aspect of rationality). 14. Philosophy (consciously depicted as the ideal life, but not of course for everyone). 15. Mind (a creative principle of order). 16. Civilization. 17. The community. 18. Its intelligent self-knowledge. 19. Law and order. 20. Measure or the mean (its absence is disastrous). 21. The form of good (the principle of the best). 22. The comprehensive or composite life (including beauty, goodness and truth, holiness, *sophrosyne*, justice, courage, wisdom). 23. The preservation and wellbeing of the whole (the subordination of part to whole is one of Plato's principles). 24. God (there are problems over Plato's theology, but the divine is a living principle of value). Lodge's point is that we must not oversimplify: passages can be found in Plato which seem to exalt and extol each of these. His last words are a good summary of Plato's values.

> Our final conclusion is thus that the highest good for the universe consists in the ideal functioning of the whole so as to realize the maximum of value-potentiality inherent in its elements, and that the highest good for a particular human being consists in so living as to constitute a consciously

organic portion of this whole, and, in so living, to realize his
own deepest happiness and well-being.

Aristotle

Aristotle (384-322 BC), 'the master of those who know' (said Dante),
was a doctor's son from the outskirts of the Greek world. He came to
Athens to study with Plato. Plato nicknamed him 'The Brain', and said
that where others needed the spur he needed the rein. When Plato
died in 347 Aristotle, after twenty years, left Athens for some fruitful
biological researches in Asia Minor and on the island of Lesbos, then
in 342 accepted an invitation to tutor Alexander, later known as the
Great. With Alexander's succession Aristotle returned to Athens to
teach. On Alexander's death, bearing the fate of Socrates in mind, he
withdrew 'to save the Athenians from sinning a second time against
philosophy'.

His supreme achievement was in the biological sciences, but his
genius was far-reaching, and he became authoritative in many fields.
Several works on ethics have come down to us. *Magna Moralia* was
probably by a later follower, and *On Virtues and Vices* is an altogether
later work of syncretism, blending the views of different thinkers. But
Ethics according to Eudemus and *Ethics according to Nicomachus* are
authentic pictures of his thought at different periods as recorded or
edited by different students. Nicomachus is fuller and more mature.
Ethics (in this version) is accessible, readable, clear, entertaining and
challenging. It is, said one scholar, 'an *aperient* book'.

Aristotle plunges straight in. 'Every science and every subject,
every action and every choice appears to aim at some good; so the
Good has been well defined as the object at which all things aim'
(*Nicomachean Ethics* 1094 a 1). There are many limited targets, but
the goal is agreed to be happiness (*eudaimonia*, with overtones of
'blessedness' and of 'success'). It is not pleasure (merely bestial) or
honour (leaving us at the mercy of others' opinions). Even *arete* can
be found with inactivity or misery. Wealth is not an end. He touches
on his eventual answer, contemplation, but goes on to examine the
function of a human being: 'an activity of the *psyche* in a manner
conforming with or at least not opposed to reason' (ibid. 1098 a 7).

Arete then, which we may render 'virtue', provided we note that
it embraces intellectual and moral excellences, 'is a fixed disposition
involving choice; it consists in a mean relative to us, which is rationally

Fig. 8. Aristotle.

determined, that is, as an intelligent man would determine it' (1106 b 36). This is filled with good sense. *Arete* is a disposition, a firm attitude of mind. I do not ask 'Shall I tell a lie?' each time I speak or 'Shall I commit adultery?' each time I meet a woman. The doctrine of the mean was illustrated by a table, of which the following are a few examples.

Field	Excess	Virtue	Defect
Fears and their absence	Rashness	Courage	Cowardice
Giving and getting money	Vulgarity	Magnificence	Meanness
Honour and dishonour	Vanity	Nobility	Ignobility
Anger	Hot temper	Good temper	Indifference
Social entertainment	Buffoonery	Wittiness	Clodhopperliness
Emotions	Shamelessness	Modesty	Shamefacedness

The mean is not arithmetical: courage is closer to rashness than to cowardice. Furthermore, right action looks like an extreme to those at the opposite extreme. The brave man appears rash to the cowardly and cowardly to the rash. The mean may vary with circumstances: moral virtue demands an activity at the right time, in the right conditions, towards the right people, for the right purpose, in the right manner (ibid. 1106 a 21). There are areas in which it is not to be applied. There is no mean in adultery: it is not possible to commit adultery with the right woman, at the right time, in the right manner (ibid. 1107 a 16). And while virtue is in essence and definition a mean, in value it is an extreme, as the bull's eye is the centre of a target, but scores the highest points.

Praise and blame attach to voluntary actions, pardon and pity to involuntary. Choice, a deliberate reaching out for things within our power (ibid. 1113 a 10), is an essential part of virtue. Aristotle, unlike Plato, in whose writings the several virtues tend to blend and blur, distinguishes carefully between them. For him the crown of the virtues is *megalopsychia*, greatness of *psyche*. We have no word for it, and do not greatly admire what we understand of it. We find such a man's nobility pompous: he does not speak ill of others except when he wants to be deliberately insulting; he prefers uselessly beautiful possessions to those that are useful or valuable; his movements are slow, his voice deep, his speech deliberate. The Victorians understood Aristotle here better than we do.

The fifth book discusses justice, *dikaiosyne*, and has been called 'a paradigm of philosophy' in its careful distinctions. Aristotle notes the loose use of the word for moral virtue in general, but its particular use is in social relationships involving gain or loss. Justice may be distributive, remedial or commercial. Distributive justice is the distribution of resources in proportion to desert; we must not forget that the Greek citizen regarded himself as a kind of shareholder in the state. Remedial justice does not act in proportion to merit, and is no respecter of persons; it tries to right wrongs. Commercial justice is the exchange of services, with money as a convenient intermediary; and it does not work by strict equality. He goes on to identify just action, somewhat implausibly, as a mean between committing and suffering injustice, and to draw important distinctions, as between natural and conventional justice,or in terms of the inner springs of action, which lead him to distinguish between accidental death, manslaughter, justifiable homicide, and murder. An important discussion of equity, 'a rectification of law where it is defective because of its generality' (ibid. 1137 b 27), has influenced the development of law.

Aristotle does not neglect the moral virtues, but he also has a strong interest in the intellectual virtues. If moral virtue arises from rational choice, then intellectual virtue is of primary importance. Within the intellect we can distinguish two faculties, one concerned with knowledge and one with deliberation and choice. Both are concerned with truth: one is theoretical, the other practical. Aristotle identifies and discusses five intellectual virtues which lead to truth: scientific knowledge, technical expertise (often, but misleadingly, rendered 'art'), practical good sense (*phronesis*), rational intuition, and theoretical wisdom (*sophia*). The distinctions are admirably drawn, and there is an extended discussion of *phronesis*. It is not possible to be good without phronesis, or to have *phronesis* without moral virtue: the two co-operate. Moral virtue ensures the rightness of the goal, *phronesis* the rightness of the means. But wisdom is more fundamental than *phronesis*.

Aristotle's treatment of internal conflict has deservedly attracted much attention in recent years. We have no precise English word for his *akrasia*: 'incontinence' is misleading, 'unrestraint' is hardly English, 'weakness of will' perhaps is as close as we can get. His discussion overemphasizes the role of reason in action, and underemphasizes the conflict of desires. He does not use the phrase 'practical syllogism', but in his book it is the rational conclusion of 'Everything sweet is pleasant' combined with 'This is sweet' which leads to the action of eating, and overrides 'Everything containing sugar is fattening' and 'This contains sugar'. To know, desire and do the right is virtue, to desire the wrong and know and do the right is strength of will, to know the right and desire and do the wrong is weakness of will, to be ignorant of the right and desire and do the wrong is vice.

Aristotle has a somewhat fragmentary discussion of pleasure, and a major monograph on friendship, an indispensable requisite of life (ibid. 1155 a 3). He finally turns to happiness as the goal of human life (ibid. 1176 a 30). It is not a state or disposition but a self-contained activity, exercising the highest part of our being, the intellect, in accordance with the highest virtue, theoretical wisdom or *sophia*. Happiness, in short, is contemplation. Furthermore, we should not set our thoughts on the ephemeral, but as far as possible ought to seek immortality. The life of moral virtue is too dependent on externals to offer full happiness. But Aristotle, whose down-to-earth common sense sometimes rebels against his theory, cannot deny the philosopher external well-being: he compromises by suggesting that his needs are less than those of others.

Some passages

(a)   *Dikaiosyne* consists in not transgressing what is established by *nomos* in the city in which one is a citizen. A man can therefore use *dikaiosyne* in a manner most advantageous to himself if he upholds the *nomoi* when in the presence of witnesses, and upholds the edicts of *physis* when on his own. The edicts of the *nomoi* are artificial, those of *physis* are essential.

(ANTIPHON (a sophist), *fr.* 44)

(b)   The Macedonians think it good (*kalon*) for girls to have love affairs and sexual experience before marriage, but disgraceful (*aischron*) after marriage; to the Greeks both are disgraceful.

(*Twofold Arguments* 2.12)

(c)   According to *physis* everything is more shameful (*aischron*) in so far as it is more evil (*kakon*), for example suffering injustice. Committing injustice is more *aischron* only by *nomos*.

(Callicles in PLATO, *Gorgias* 483 A)

(d)   Anyway I think that he (Socrates) with words like these kept his associates from impious, unjust and shameful acts, not merely before other people's eyes, but when on their own, since they came to the conclusion that the gods would always observe their actions.

(XENOPHON, *Memorabilia* 1.4.19)

(e)   I assume that there are such things as absolute beauty (*kalon*), good (*agathon*), largeness and so on...I am further clear that if anything is beautiful besides beauty itself, the only reason it is beautiful is that it shares in that beauty.

(Socrates in PLATO, *Phaedo* 100 B-C)

(f)   May we not then affirm that that man is happy who acts in accordance with the fullness of *arete*, and is adequately provided with external goods.

(ARISTOTLE, *Nicomachean Ethics* 1101 a 15-8)

Brief comments

(a) A typical sophistic passage, reflecting the debate between *nomos* and *physis*. It is possibly true that *dikaiosyne* originated in following the normal practice of society, whether embodied in law or not. (*Nomoi* are probably the laws, but *nomos* here is wider.) But there was also a view which made *dike* more ultimate. *Physis* is 'nature'. This may apply to physical necessity. If I jump off a cliff I will be killed. This contrasts with moral choice. But *physis* of my 'inward nature' is harder. It is all very well saying that the edicts of *physis* are essential, but what does it mean? Unless I am technically a kleptomaniac I can control my impulses to steal. So some claimed *nomos* as an unjustifiable infringement of *physis*, others saw it as a civilizing control.

(b) This comes from an anonymous sophistic work, and is typical of the fruits of human geography and anthropology in the period, an observation that different moral values exist in different parts. This may be taken to the conclusion that all moral standards are subjective, but need not be. It will be noticed that the standard is public opinion; it will also be noticed that the moral standards of the girls are laid down by the males.

(c) Another sophistic view, with the *nomos-physis* antithesis forcefully spelled out. What is new in the passage as compared with the others is the use of *kakon* to mean 'unpleasant *for me*', 'damaging *to me*'. There is no ethical content. It is almost a reversion to Homeric usage.

(d) Xenophon depicts Socrates as a pietistic moralist, nowhere more clearly than here. His Socrates is a platitudinous preacher, not a shrewd, questioning searcher of souls. (Socrates, incidentally, was executed because his words did not keep some of his associates from violent and tyrannical acts; political orators make this clear: 'You executed Socrates the sophist, because he was clearly responsible for the education of Critias, one of the Thirty anti-democratic leaders' said Aeschines (1.173).) The three categories of wrong acts are interesting, corresponding to offences against the gods, against the 'way', and against public opinion. The ultimate sanction is divine punishment. Critias (one of those associates who went his own way) made a dramatic character suggest that the gods were an invention to provide such a sanction.

(e) This is an early statement of the Theory of Forms, and represents a point where Plato is putting his own conclusions into the mouth of Socrates. True reality is in the changeless eternal Forms, known with the mind. The examples are aesthetic, moral (but wider in scope) and material: the first two involve value-judgements, largeness does not. Objects in this world are imperfect, changing, lacking durability, perceived through the senses. Such qualities as they have come from participation in or imitation of the Forms.

(f) From the first book of Aristotle's *Nicomachean Ethics*. It is not exactly the final conclusion, where contemplation is ranked above moral virtue as a higher happiness, less dependent on external circumstances. But *arete*, here moral virtue, does bring happiness; it must be exercised in action. Aristotle, however, remains middle-class enough to require for happiness a measure of external goods.

Chapter 5
The Hellenistic Age

Historical background

Philip II ruled Macedonia from 359 to 336 BC, and by a combination of military ability, skilled diplomacy and bribery expanded the power of this kingdom on the outskirts of the Greek world to take in mainland Greece. He was assassinated at the age of 46 and succeeded by his greater son Alexander, who two years later began the stupendous expedition which brought down the power of the Persian Empire, drew Asia Minor, Syria and Palestine, Egypt, Mesopotamia, Iran, and areas beyond, into his dominion. He had been encouraged by Isocrates to lead the Greeks in unity against the 'barbarians' or non-Greeks; he had been taught by Aristotle that foreigners were by nature slaves. But *de facto* he had to use non-Greeks, and he found Greeks with feet of clay and Asiatics whom he could trust, and conceived at least a partnership between Greeks and Persians. When Greeks, who tended to be racist, protested 'You have made the Persians your kinsmen', he replied 'I make you all my kinsmen.'

Alexander died very young. No single man could hold his empire together. But men who had been pawns at his side now became monarchs in their own right. The clock could not be put back. The day of the wholly independent city-state was gone. The empire broke into warring kingdoms, still gigantic by the old standards. Out of the jockeyings for power emerged three major powers. One was Macedon, which for the most part exercised hegemony over mainland Greece. The second was Egypt, where a shrewd officer named Ptolemy established a Greek dynasty, securing Alexander's body to give him prestige, having a magnificent capital in the new city of Alexandria, and using administrative genius to give his realm a firm economic foundation. The third was Syria with its new capital Antioch-on-the-Orontes, from where Seleucus exercised power over Alexander's Asian conquests: Seleucus had a high reputation for integrity, and it is notable that he did not repudiate his Persian wife. Pergamum in Asia Minor seceded in 282 and formed a fourth kingdom, conquering the Celts of the interior, and establishing itself as champion of Hellenism against 'barbarism', and setting up as an academic and cultural centre to rival Athens and Alexandria. Further east, on the borders of the Indian subcontinent, Bactria became virtually independent, but retained Greek culture even when one of the rulers was converted to Buddhism.

But cosmopolis did not annihilate the *polis*: it changed the backcloth against which the *polis* played out its drama. People still belonged to a *polis*, and thought in those terms. There were new foundations, and old ones restored. Priene was one of the latter, its population about 4000, its streets aligned N-S or E-W, with temples, theatre, city-centre, council-chamber, athletics track and changing-rooms. Even after Rome conquered the Greek world the *polis* retained its centrality for the life of its citizens. Rome fostered this pride in one's own locality, while holding out the prospect of citizenship of Rome as well.

The ideal ruler

The titles taken by the kings show something of the character they wished to display to their subjects. Thus we find among the Ptolemies Soter (Liberator or Saviour), Philadelphus (Brother-lover), Euergetes (Benefactor), Philopator (Father-lover), Philometor (Mother-lover), Epiphanes (God manifest). In the Seleucid dynasty we have Nicator (Victor), Callinicus (Glorious in victory) as well as Soter, Philopator and Epiphanes. The rulers of Pergamum include a Soter, Philadelphus, and Philometor Euergetes.

Some kind of ruler-cult was usual. Alexander had taken the decision to appear as a divine king: in Egypt this was almost inevitable. The mood of the times was shown when in 307 BC Demetrius 'the Besieger' entered Athens and was welcomed with a hymn:

> The greatest, the dearest of the gods
> Are here in our city...
> He is here in gladness, handsome, smiling
> As a god should be...
> Other gods are far away
> Or cannot hear,
> Or do not exist at all, or care nothing for us.
> You are present; we can see you,
> Not carved in wood or stone, but real.
> To you we pray.

First bring us peace – we love you dearly –
You have the power.

The rulers were expected to provide the boons formerly expected
from the Olympian gods. We can see an emphasis on peace, victory,
security, family solidarity. 'Benefactor' was a special title. 'The kings
of the Gentiles lord it over them, and those with power are called their
Benefactors', said Jesus. 'Not so with you' (Luke 22.25). He does not
mean that he does not want his followers to be beneficent, but he
wants them to serve, not to condescend.

A word of special commendation was *philanthropia*. Of itself it
means 'love of human beings'. It appears first in the fifth century. The
Hippocratic precept 'Where there is love of human beings there is
love of medical science' shows a high ethical use. Theophrastus,
successor to Aristotle, says 'We affirm that all humans are in fact kin
to one another. We have a common *philanthropia*' (Porphyry, *On
Abstinence* 3.25; Stobaeus, 2.7.13). But it was a natural word to apply
to gods or demigods favourable to humans, to Prometheus or Hermes
or Eros or Heracles, and so it passed to the potentates with the same
sense of condescension. The historian Polybius (5.11.16) speaks of
kingly duties as benefactions combined with *philanthropia*. Its
appearance in the books of the Maccabees shows that it has become
a formal attribute of sovereignty (2 Maccabees 9.27, 13.23, 14.9).

Utopian visions

The visionary creation of Utopias speaks of dissatisfaction with the
present and an aspiring search for values lost or never attained, and
the Hellenistic age was a great period for Utopias; more (though some
scholars deny it), they play some part, if only a small one, in shaping
practical politics.

Zeno, the founder of the Stoics, as a young man wrote of a
community of the wise, linked by the power of Love (*Eros*), exercised
freely with no room for jealousy or family rivalries, with no temples,
lawcourts, gymnasia, money or commerce. The unit would be the
polis, but the city-states would be part of a single universal order; the
citizens would be members of one flock and subject to one common
law, regarding all people as their fellow-citizens.

Euhemerus was a rationalist who believed that gods were simply
humans from the past. He threw these ideas into a kind of Utopian
novel, in which Nature is all perfection, and an ideal society, though

divided into three classes (priests and administrators, farmers, soldiers and herdsmen), is free from economic privilege, industrialism and slavery. Private property is virtually abolished and there is no money.

An eccentric brother of Euhemerus's patron Cassander meantime founded a city called Uranopolis, City of Heaven; the citizens were not Uranopolitae, Citizens of Uranopolis, but Uranidae, Children of Heaven. Alexarchus invented a new language for his city, and identified himself with the Sun as all-ruler. But we know too little of this strange experiment.

Shortly after 250 BC a man named Iambulus wrote a Utopian novel about a traveller, sent off by African Negroes ('Ethiopians') to secure them peace and prosperity, and reaching the Islands of the Sun, where live the Children of the Sun. These people enjoy physical equality (including unusual and implausible physical features). Equality and universalism are the rules of the community. Wives and children are held in common: there is no private property; they share out the work. There is no slavery. Life-style is simple. Education is valued. At the age of 150 they commit euthanasial suicide. Some of these ideas passed into Stoic circles, and, through his tutor Sphaerus, touched Cleomenes III who essayed in Sparta a return to the old way of life, and, through another Stoic, Blossius, touched the Gracchi at Rome, and Aristonicus of Pergamum who aroused the serfs to form a community which they called the City of the Sun.

An oracle valued by Cleopatra VII of Egypt spoke of the hope of peace and blessing for Asia and Europe, with Nature cooperating supernaturally, and law, righteousness, concord, love, trust, friendship with the stranger flourishing, and poverty, compulsion, lawlessness, carping, envy, anger, folly, murder, strife, conflict, night-robbery and every evil vanishing (*Sibylline* Oracles 3.367-80). It may have been propaganda only – but at least it was worth putting out as propaganda.

From these Utopian visions we receive a sense of a world dominated by violence, injustice and privilege, with the rich getting richer and the poor poorer. The values these writers foster are peace and concord (*homonoia*), equality, justice. For the Utopians the all-seeing sun becomes the symbol of justice.

The search for self-sufficiency

The late Gilbert Murray in a familiar phrase which he derived from the historian J.B. Bury, described the Hellenistic Age as characterized by 'the failure of nerve'. The old gods had failed to save. But individuals who had felt that they had some say in the independent *polis* were now in the grip of world-forces beyond their control. The armies marched hither and thither. Any moment they might be killed, or enslaved, or lose their all.

What power was in control? Perhaps Chance, *Tyche*. The Aristotelian Demetrius of Phalerum could say 'The last fifty years show the violence of Fortune.' Even Theophrastus wrote 'Fortune, not counsel, guides human affairs.' A character in a play by the dramatist Menander, always an index of the times, says

> Stop blathering about will. Human will
> Adds up to nothing. Fortune's will –
> Call it divine spirit or intelligent will –
> It is that pilots the universe, steers
> And saves. Mortal forethought is gas
> And gaiters. Listen to me. You won't regret it.
> All we will, all we say, all we do
> Is Fortune; we simply add our signatures.

Others thought the stars determined our destiny.

Individuals in the Hellenistic world were crying out 'Where shall security be found?' 'How can I be saved?' – not in terms of an emotional religiosity, but simply 'How can I be safe?'

The question was already being asked in the fourth century, and the answer looked for in some kind of self-sufficiency, *autarkeia*, autarky (not to be confused with autarchy, which means personal rule, autocracy). Aristotle found the contemplative life the most self-sufficient of all, though even the philosopher needs food and drink and health. Beneficence needs someone on whom to practise it; justice or courage cannot be exercised without some external factors. But the philosopher can contemplate on his own.

The great exponent of autarky was prominent in the third quarter of the fourth century. This was Diogenes, nicknamed the Dog, whose followers were called 'Dog-philosophers' or Cynics, a word which has changed its meaning. From about 340 to 320 Diogenes went round the Greek world, practising an extreme form of autarky (Aldous Huxley's term 'non-attachment' comes as near to it as we can), an itinerant preacher without citizenship, home or possessions, defying convention, 'putting false coinage out of circulation'. He renounced citizenship. He could not be taxed or conscribed. Faced with the ancient equivalent of customs and immigration, he declared 'I am a citizen of the universe'; in a skit by the Syrian satirical writer Lucian he declared that he came from 'everywhere'. He was 'as free as a bird, unconstrained by law, undisturbed by politicians' (Maximus of Tyre 36.6). His follower Crates called himself 'a citizen of Diogenes' (Diogenes Laertius, 6.93). He renounced home except for a large earthenware jar in which he could shelter. He renounced possessions except for a satchel, and, in old age, a staff: even cup and bowl he threw away after seeing a boy eat off a slice of bread, and drink from cupped hands.

The means to autarky were *askesis* and *ponos*. *Askesis*, which gives us our word 'ascetic', denotes training, practice, discipline. *Ponos* means labour, toil, hardship: Heracles was the typical Cynic saint. Diogenes saw the two as interlinked. Excellence in craftsmanship or music or athletics is attained only by hard work and disciplined training. So it is with moral excellence. There was nothing very new in the cult of *askesis* and *ponos*. It had been practised in Sparta for centuries; the educationalist Isocrates repeatedly stressed both. But the fanatical intensity of the training was new. 'In summer he used to roll over in the scorching sand, in winter to embrace the snow-covered statues, using every means of self-discipline' (Diogenes Laertius 6.23). Like the poet A.E. Housman's Shropshire Lad, Diogenes trained for ill and not for good. Banishment could not touch him, nor confiscation of goods, nor poverty, nor torture.

His celebrated flouting of convention contains something of self-advertisement as when he entered a theatre while the spectators were coming out, to demonstrate that he deliberately chose to be different. But his refusal to be bound by *aidos* and *aischron* was in itself an assertion of an internal standard of morality against an external one, an assertion of *physis* against *nomos*. He would eat and perform sexual acts (such as masturbation) in public; if they were all right in private they were all right in public (Diogenes Laertius 6.69). It is the extreme antithesis of a shame-culture.

The Cynic attitude may be further exemplified by some sayings of Teles, a century later, as preserved by John Stobaeus, an anthologist of the fifth century AD. Get rid of your possessions: they are only on deposit. Find your food in the roads and rivers. One cloak will serve you; double your summer cloak and you have a winter cloak. Nation, tribe, the extended family – these are nothing. What do you lose in exile? Anxiety about dependents! Your friend may die, even your children: that's no reason for killing yourself. 'Fortune is like a dramatist who designs a number of parts – the shipwrecked man, the poor man, the exile, the king, the beggar. What the good man has to do is to play well any part for which Fortune casts him.' 'That was a splendid saying of the skipper, "All right, Poseidon, but she's on course?" So a good man may say to Fortune, "All right, but you're sinking a man not a coward."' Non-attachment may be a self-centred philosophy, but it is not ignoble.

The Cynics are the extreme examples of the pursuit of autarky, but it is there in all the Hellenistic thinkers. The Stoics, and even the Neoplatonists, treat pity as a vice, a sickness of the soul, a weakness of the tearful eye; for if you are liable to pity, your peace of mind depends on what happens to another, and that is out of your control. You are no longer self-sufficient. Again Epicurus, who disliked the Cynics and called them 'enemies of Greece' (Diogenes Laertius, 10.8) wrote in praise of self-sufficiency to Menoeceus:

> We regard autarky as a great good, not with a view to always making do with a little, but to finding a little sufficient if we have not got a lot, frankly realizing that it is the people who least need luxury who enjoy it most, and only gewgaws are hard to come by; that which is natural is readily accessible. Plain fare gives as much pleasure as an expensive menu, when once the pain of want has been removed. Bread and water offer the keenest pleasure when a hungry man tackles them. So to accustom oneself to a simple, inexpensive regime provides all that is needful for health, and enables a person to face more readily the inescapable demands of life. It places us in a better position when we do occasionally come on luxuries. It enables us to face fortune fearlessly.
>
> (ibid. 10.130-1)

In a fragment (70) he called it the greatest of all riches. Its greatest fruit is freedom (*fr.* lxxvii).

Epicureans

This may lead us to the Epicureans. Epicurus (341-270 BC), an Athenian born in Samos, was founder of one of the two new schools of thought which arose to meet the new situation and dominated the

Hellenistic Age. Epicurean philosophy might be summed up in twelve Greek words, the so-called Fourfold Cure:

> There is nothing to fear in God.
> There is nothing to feel in death.
> Good can be procured.
> Evil can be endured.

The beginning and end of happiness is pleasure (Diogenes Laertius, 10.128): in that, Epicurus is a hedonist. But he practises a hedonistic calculus and chooses those actions which involve the greatest excess of pleasure over pain, or (as he tends to pessimism) the least excess of pain over pleasure. Pleasure of the *psyche* is superior to physical pleasure, and consists in not being shaken, freedom from disturbance, *ataraxia*, peace of mind. The things which disturb our peace of mind are fears and desires outrunning their natural course. Fears are dispelled by a scientific understanding of the atomic structure of the universe so that nothing exists but atoms and void. Among other things this teaches us that gods do not intervene in human affairs, death is the painless dissolution of our atomic structure, and there is no life beyond. Desires which are natural and necessary are easily satisfied; if they are natural but unnecessary, they should be controlled; if they are neither natural nor necessary, they should be dismissed. Examples would be the desire for food or drink; the desire for good food or drink; the desire for public fame, political power, military conquest. 'Live a private life', said Epicurus in a famous phrase (*fr.* 551). The practical side of this was withdrawal to the Garden: this was initially the grounds of his own house where the fellowship met, but it symbolized the withdrawal from public life. Epicurus found room in his philosophy for the traditional virtues. 'It is impossible to live pleasurably, without living wisely, well and justly' (Diogenes Laertius, 10.132).

One other positive value he exalted was friendship (*philia*). Indeed we have a record of Epicurus rebuking Stilpo, a thinker influenced by the Cynics, for saying that the wise man, being self-sufficient, needed no friends (Seneca, *Letters* 9.1). Friendship starts from the need for help but it is desirable for its own sake (*fr.* xxiii). That the calculating justification for friendship in terms of self-interest falls away is clear in three astonishing sayings. 'Of all the things which wisdom acquires to produce the blessedness of the complete life, by far the greatest is the possession of friendship' (*fr.* 148, 27). 'Friendship goes dancing round the world proclaiming to us all to awake to the praise of happiness' (*Add. fr.* 52 from a Vatican MS). 'The noble person exercises himself above all in wisdom and friendship – the first a mortal good, the second an immortal one' (*Add. fr.* 78). This last is a colossal paradox. Epicurean philosophy sometimes seems cold, but when clothed with values of this kind it is warming.

The Stoics

The other great Hellenistic way of life was the Stoic, and it was poles apart from the Epicurean. An epigram said that the Epicurean would not enter public life unless compelled to do so, the Stoic would enter public life unless circumstances prevented him (Seneca, *Dialogues* 8.3.2). Their founder was the exalted moralist Zeno of Citium (335-263 BC), who held that moral virtue is the only real good, moral weakness the only real evil. All else is 'indifferent', some preferable, other things being equal, some not, but never to be pursued for their own sakes. The wise man is always in possession of the only true good, virtue, and nothing can deprive him of it. Zeno was succeeded by a religious genius named Cleanthes, and he by the great systematizer Chrysippus. After Chrysippus the essence of the philosophy did not change, though later generations modified some of their more extreme positions to suit the down-to-earth Romans.

The Stoics were pantheists. All is not merely in the hands of God, all is God and God is all. Alexander Pope was really expressing a Stoic view when he wrote into his *Essay on Man* a passage beginning

> All are but parts of one stupendous whole,
> Whose body, Nature is, and God the soul;

and ending

> And, spite of Pride, in erring Reason's spite,
> One truth is clear, "Whatever IS, is RIGHT."

(267-94)

Pantheism led to a doctrine of resignation. Our destinies, our actions are determined by an almighty Providence. We are pawns in a divine game of chess. We may be sacrificed in the opening moves or we may win through to being queens. Either way we are part of the divine strategy. Our fate is determined by God. What he does not determine is how we accept it. So a Greek Stoic of the Roman period, an ex-slave named Epictetus, who was lame, says

> Must my leg be the object of blame? Slave! Do you, for one
> wretched leg, find fault with the cosmos? Will you not
> gladly surrender it for the whole?
>
> (1.12.24)

The resignation is impressive. But questions remain. Because a small imperfection remains an imperfection, which has to be explained; because 'I dislike what I fancy I feel'; because it is his leg in a way in which it is not quite his universe. But Epictetus is essentially a man of faith not a logician.

> What else can I do, a lame old man, but sing hymns to God?
> If I were a nightingale I would do as a nightingale; if a swan,
> as a swan. As it is, I am a rational being, and I ought to
> praise God: this is my job, and I perform it. I will not desert
> this post as long as I am allowed to keep it – and I charge
> you to join in the same song.
>
> (1.16.20-1)

The Stoics were famous for their paradoxes. The Roman Cicero explained six of them: that only what is *kalon* is *agathon* (an action must be right, honourable and virtuous); that *arete* (here virtue) is *autarkes* (sufficient in itself) for happiness; that moral failures are equal and moral successes are equal (it is no use saying of an illegitimate baby that it is only a small one); that everyone who lacks *phronesis* is mad; that only the wise man is free, and everyone who lacks *phronesis* is a slave (as in Epictetus's self-rebuke above); that the wise man alone is rich (*Paradoxes of the Stoics*). Elsewhere Cicero teases the Stoics for these paradoxes, and it was here that some modifications were introduced. The Stoics could defend the paradox that you were either a 'wise man' or a 'fool', a 'king' or a 'slave'. You are, after all, drowned six inches below the water's surface as surely as full fathom five; when the gates are shut at the opera you do not get in whether you are left in front of the queue or right at the rear. But for the Romans the Stoics introduced the concept of personal progress: you have, so to say, more chance of getting in next time.

The mystery religions

A mystery is, quite literally, something you keep mum about, a secret revealed only to initiates and not to be revealed to others. It follows that we have no certain knowledge of the central facts of the mystery religions, though we can make informed guesses and deductions.

They are important in earlier periods. They spread widely during the period of 'the failure of nerve'. As the old religions failed, the power of the *polis* was dimmed and with it the corporate religion which had been a vital dimension of civic life; people looked for individual salvation.

The most celebrated of the mystery-cults went a long way further back, the cult of Demeter and Kore (the Maid) at Eleusis. The myth of the rape of the Corn-Maiden by the god of the underworld, and her mother's anguish, a myth of the summer drought and the burial of the seed-corn underground till the time for planting, retains power, and symbolizes life after death. 'The ceremonies', said the Roman Cicero, 'are called initiations, and we recognize in them the first principles of living. We have gained from them the way of living in happiness and dying with a better hope' (*Laws* 2.14.36).

Other mysteries proliferated. Kore or Persephone might have her own mysteries in South Italy and Sicily, where gold tablets have been found giving the soul instructions as to how to behave after death. The wild god of nature Dionysus had his mysteries; there were cults in the Greek cities of the bay of Naples. Orpheus, from the very fringes of the Greek world, had his. Mostly the deities concerned were exotic. On the island of Samothrace they worshipped the Cabeiri – 'the oldest of spirits', said Aelius Aristides (c. AD 117-181)– who had control of mysteries giving protection against storms. Cybele and Attis came from Asia Minor, Isis and Osiris from Egypt, Mithras from Persia, though he never made a great impact on the Greek world.

Initiation normally involved sacrifice, and practices of ritual and ethical purity. The ethical demands might not run very deep. Diogenes 'the Dog' refused initiation, remarking 'It is ridiculous if Agesilaus and Epaminondas are going to be consigned to the mire, and no-account nobodies are going to be in the Isles of the Blessed just because they have been initiated' (Diogenes Laertius, 6.39). There was a bit more to it than that, though not always very much. There might be demands of sexual chastity and ascetic living. There was a sense of unity among the initiates. The mysteries which believed in reincarnation held that the destiny in a new life was fixed by behaviour in the old incarnation. A mystical experience at a high level, the experience of enlightenment, is seldom totally divorced from a reform of life-style.

Fig. 9. Demeter.

Christianity entered the Greek world as a mystery religion. It was different in two ways. First, it cost nothing to be initiated: this is why A.D. Nock once said 'It was left to Christianity to democratize mystery.' Writing about AD 178 the Platonist Celsus complained that the Christians were from the lower classes, 'wood-workers, cobblers, laundry-workers, and the most illiterate and bucolic yokels' (Henry Chadwick's version of ORIGEN, *Against Celsus* 3.55). Second, it did make ethical demands, and that not so much in the form of a set of rules as an attitude directing action. Celsus said that Christian ethical teaching was taken from Greek philosophy, and Origen enthusiastically, as a Christian, agreed with him: in God's Providence, why not? This does less than justice to the essence of the Christian ethic, though as the Christians spread they came to accept – selectively – the rules of behaviour, first of Jews and then of Greeks. The Christian ethical stance is expressed in a word relatively unfamiliar when the Christian writers coined it, *agape*, translated 'love', but not to be confused with *eros*, passionate or possessive love, or *philia*, limited in scope and reciprocal. *Agape* denotes the ceaseless seeking of the well-being of the other, regardless of their merits or response. The Christians derived their ethic from the belief that it is the ultimate fact about the universe – 'God is *agape*' (1 John 4.8), and revealed, as they believed, in the life and death and ongoing life of Jesus. Within the circle of the initiates this was not very different from the *philia* which held together the initiates of other mysteries (John 15.12), though the pagans were impressed by its intensity, especially in the practical care for widows and orphans. But it was not confined to initiates. It reached out to others also, including persecutors, oppressors, military governments and criminals (Matthew 5.43-8). A body of teaching was handed down and led to non-violence and pacifism, simplicity of lifestyle and awareness of the danger of riches, non-judgemental attitudes, freedom from worry, care for the hungry and the thirsty and the sick, straightforwardness of speech, control of anger and sexual passion. Some scholars have held that the Christians were expecting the imminent return of Christ in glory, and this was an 'ethic of the interim', suitable to a short period only, not as a permanent way of life; but this does not appear from the Christian scriptures where it is rooted in the nature of God (Matthew 5.45; 1 John 4.8). Not that Christians at any time practised what they preached or lived up to their professions. But a commitment was there, and a uniting of religion and ethics derived from Judaism, but not previously found to such an extent among the Greeks.

Some passages

(a)   When he (Diogenes) was sunning himself...Alexander stood
       over him and said 'Ask of me anything you like.' 'Please don't
       keep the sun off me', said Diogenes.

                                            (DIOGENES LAERTIUS, 6.38)

(b)   We call pleasure the beginning and end of living the blessed
       life. We can recognize pleasure as a good which is primary and
       innate in us, and we begin every act of choice and avoidance
       from pleasure and return to it again, using our experience of it
       as the criterion of every good thing.

                                            (EPICURUS in ib. 10.128-9)

(c)   The wise man is happy even on the rack.

                                            (EPICURUS in ib. 10.118)

(d)   Lead me, Zeus, and you, Destiny,
       Wherever you decree that I shall go.
       Unhesitatingly I'll follow: yet if in sin
       I refuse, I shall still follow.

                                    (Cleanthes in EPICTETUS *Handbook* 53)

(e)   You laid the foundation-stone of self-sufficiency, Zeno.

                                    (ZENODOTUS in *Greek Anthology* 7.117)

(f)   Blessed among men on earth is he who has seen these things.
       But he who is uninitiate in the holy rites, with no lot in them,
       Is not so destined lying under spreading darkness in death.

                                    ([HOMER] *Hymn to Demeter* 479-82)

(g)   The fruit of the Spirit is *agape*, joy, peace, longsuffering, kind-
       ness, goodness, fidelity, gentleness, endurance.

                                    (PAUL Galatians 5.22)

Some comments

       (a) Diogenes, founder of the Cynics, nicknamed 'the Dog', was
an extreme exponent of autarky, who did without possessions and
limited his requirements to virtually nothing. It was natural to invent

encounters between him and the ruler of the world; this is one of the best such stories.

(b) Epicurus, founder of one of the two great new schools of Hellenistic thought, was philosophically a hedonist. He is here saying that as children we choose things which are 'nice' and avoid things which are 'nasty', and that in a more sophisticated way (calculating the pleasure and pain involved in different courses of action) this remains our guide through life. But this did not lead to a selfish immoralism: he held that there is no true pleasure in folly and immorality.

(c) This commonplace of the Hellenistic age comes a little unexpectedly from Epicurus with his philosophy of pleasure. It is an extreme statement of autarky and the triumph of ethical values over physical pain.

(d) A statement of determinism or predestination by the most religious of the Stoics. The events of our life are determined by the God who is all in all (call him Zeus or Destiny or what you will). He does not determine our assent. To refuse that assent is the one real sin. (Carlyle heard Margaret Fuller say 'I accept the universe' and rejoined 'By God, she'd better!')

(e) A much later tribute to the founder of the Stoics as establishing the greatest philosophical expression of autarky. The Stoics, less flamboyant than the Cynics, held that virtue was the only good and attainable by all. All external goods, possessions, families and the like prove matters of indifference.

(f) A 'Homeric Hymn' (not by Homer) to Demeter, the chief goddess of the Eleusinian Mysteries. It tells us (i) that the initiate is blessed in this life, (ii) that the revelation was something seen, (iii) that the initiate has a better fate than the uninitiate after death. The statement as it stands is exposed by the absence of any ethical content to the criticism that initiated rascals are better off than uninitiated saints.

(g) An early statement of the ethical content of Christianity. It will be seen that these are not so many rules to be obeyed, but revealed and received from the Spirit of the God who is identified by the Christians with *agape*, love, humanly speaking the first of those fruits. The 'virtues', except for endurance, are unlike those found in the Greek philosophers, being self-effacing.

Suggestions for Further Study

1. If you had lived in Homeric times, what moral values would you have sought to observe? Why?

2. What were the main changes of value to be discerned in the seventh and sixth centuries BC?

3. How far is the language used by Solon and later oligarchs and democrats mere words and how far does it in each case reflect genuine values?

4. Use the categories of *nomos* and *physis* to examine some social and personal values of our own times.

5. Discuss the concept of excellence.

6. Does a doctrine of reincarnation help to sustain ethical values? Is that a reason for believing it?

7. Take a closer look at the Socratic paradoxes.

8. If Plato's Theory of Forms is true, how can it relate to the 'nitty-gritty' of our ethical behaviour? On the other hand if there are no such ultimate values, do we really have any ethical direction?

9. Examine critically Aristotle's view of the supreme good.

10. How did values change in the Hellenistic age in response to historical events?

11. Is the concept of the Way ethically useful? How did the Greeks develop it?

12. Examine the meaning, development and value of the terms *kalon, sophrosyne, phronesis, aischron, philia, philanthropia, agape.*

Suggestions for Further Reading

A. Ancient authors in translation

Homer

Homer was a poet, and should preferably be read in a verse translation. The best is probably:
Lattimore, R., *The Iliad of Homer*, University of Chicago Press.
Lattimore, R., *The Odyssey of Homer*.
A prose translation which has sold well is:
Rieu, E.V., *Homer: The Iliad*, (new translation by Martin Hammond), Penguin.
Rieu, E.V., *Homer: The Odyssey*, Penguin.

Hesiod

Wender, D., *Hesiod and Theognis*, Penguin, is good.

Lyric and elegiac poets

Wender, D., *Hesiod and Theognis*, Penguin, is good for Theognis. For the rest nothing very satisfactory is available.
Barnstone, W., *Greek Lyric Poetry*, Bantam, is as good as any.

Dramatists

Grene, D. and Lattimore, R. (ed.), *The Complete Greek Tragedies*, University of Chicago Press, is the best collection. Most of the tragedies are available in Penguins in adequate but sometimes undistinguished versions.
Vellacott, P., *Aeschylus: Prometheus and Other Plays*, Penguin.
Vellacott, P., *Aeschylus: The Oresteian Trilogy*, Penguin.
Fagles, R., *The Oresteia*, Penguin (which is more poetical).
Watling, E.F., *Sophocles: The Theban Plays*, Penguin.
Watling, E.F., *Sophocles: Electra and Other Plays*, Penguin.

Vellacott, P., *Euripides: Alcestis and Other Plays*, Penguin.
Vellacott, P., *Euripides: Medea and Other Plays*, Penguin.
For comedy most of Aristophanes is available in lively contemporary
American translation by William Arrowsmith and Douglas Parker in
Mentor Books. See also:
> Barrett, D., *Aristophanes: The Frogs and Other Plays*, Penguin.
> Fitts, D., *The Lysistrata of Aristophanes*, Faber and Faber.

For Menander:
> Vellacott, P., *Menander: Plays and Fragments*, Penguin.

Historians

Selincourt, A. de, *Herodotus: The Histories*, Penguin.
> Warner, R., *Thucydides: History of the Peloponnesian War*.

Both these Penguins are reliable.

Orators

Saunders, A.N.W., *Greek Political Oratory*, Penguin, is a useful
selection.

Philosophers

The early philosophers can be conveniently studied in:
> Barnes, J., *Early Greek Philosophy*, Penguin.

There is a one-volume complete Plato:
> Hamilton, E. and Cairns, H. (ed.), *Plato: Collected Dialogues*,
Bollingen series, Pantheon Books.

Penguins provide:
> Tredennick, H., *Plato: The Last Days of Socrates*, Penguin, which
contains *Apology, Crito, Phaedo*.
> Lee, H.D.P., *Plato: The Republic*, Penguin, though many people
prefer the more fluent and readable
> Cornford, F.M., *The Republic of Plato*, Oxford.

Also:
> Guthrie, W.K.C., *Plato: Protagoras and Meno*, Penguin.
> Hamilton, W., *Plato: Gorgias*, Penguin.
> Hamilton, W., *Plato: The Symposium*, Penguin.
> Lee, H.D.P., *Plato: Timaeus*, Penguin.

Saunders, T.J., *Plato: The Laws*, Penguin.

For Aristotle there is a useful one-volume selection
Bambrough, R., *The Philosophy of Aristotle*, Mentor.

The two most important works available for our purposes are
Thomson, J.A., *The Ethics of Aristotle*, Penguin.
Sinclair, T.A. (rev. T.J. Saunders), *Aristotle: The Politics*,
Penguin.

Also useful is:
Lloyd, G.E.R., *Hippocratic Writings*, Penguin.

B. Modern works

General

Adkins, Arthur W.H., *Merit and Responsibility: A Study in Greek Values*, Clarendon Press, 1960. A most important and original study, which revolutionized attitudes to Greek views of moral responsibility. The survey ranges from Homer to Aristotle, but does not cover the later period. It mainly uses literature and philosophy as its sources (it is difficult to do otherwise). It is scholarly and full of insights.
Adkins, A.W.H., *Moral Values and Political Behaviour in Ancient Greece*, Chatto and Windus, 1972. A useful reprise and rethink, covering slightly different ground, and written more generally. An important complementary study.
Dover, Sir Kenneth, *Greek Popular Morality in the time of Plato and Aristotle*, Blackwell, 1974. Brilliant, learned and subtle, and not at all easy.
Ferguson, John, *Moral Values in the Ancient World*, Methuen, 1958. This was a pioneering study, inadequate in some ways, especially in its treatment of Homeric society. Some reviewers found it too 'preachy' in the treatment of the Christian value of *agape* at the end. In between it collects useful material not easily to be found elsewhere.
Frisch, H., *Might and Right in Antiquity*, Copenhagen: Gyldendal, 1949. An important book by the Minister of Education in Denmark, treating individual words with great care.

Greene, W.C., *Moira: Fate, Good and Evil in Greek Thought*, Harper and Row, 1963. A highly original treatment, thorough and exciting.

Lloyd-Jones, H., *The Justice of Zeus*, University of California Press, 1971. A study of *Dike*, arguing for its link with religion and its upholding by the gods.

Historical background

Burn, A.R., *The Pelican History of Greece*, Penguin Books, 1966. A very convenient one-volume history, readable and reliable.

Bury, J.B., (rev. R. Meiggs, 1960) *A History of Greece*, Macmillan, 1951. Still in many ways the best comprehensive one-volume history. Bury was a great historian who also wrote well: Russell Meiggs did a brilliant piece of updating.

The Cambridge Ancient History, vols 1-9, CUP, 1923-32. This gives the most comprehensive coverage, but much of it is over sixty years old, and we have today different emphases, as well as fresh factual knowledge. The older volumes are steadily being replaced on an even larger scale.

Davies, J.K., *Democracy and Classical Greece*, Fontana, 1978. Up-to-date and excellent on social history, but not easy as an introduction.

Hammond, N.G.L., *A History of Greece*, OUP, 1959. The most comprehensive recent single-volume history, a little unexciting, and perhaps too inclined to 'swallow' the ancient sources.

Murray, O., *Early Greece*, Fontana, 1980. A really exciting and clear account of the early period.

1. Homeric values

Finley, M.I., *The World of Odysseus* 2nd ed., Chatto and Windus, 1956. A valuable account of society as depicted in *The Odyssey*.

Wace, A.J.B. and Stubbings, F.H. (ed.) *A Companion to Homer*, Macmillan, 1962. A large book covering all manner of aspects of the Homeric poems and Homeric society in the light of the major discoveries of archaeology and anthropology during this century.

2. From shame to guilt

Bowra, C.M., *Early Greek Elegists*, Heffer, 1960.

Bowra, C.M., *Greek Lyric Poetry* 2nd ed., OUP, 1960. The standard introduction in English.

Burn, A.R., *The Lyric Age of Greece*, Arnold, 1960. A general history covering 750-510 BC and including literature and thought.

Dodds, E.R., *The Greeks and the Irrational*, University of California Press, 1951. Highly original and influential.

Norwood, G., *Pindar*, University of California Press, 1945. The Sather Classical Lectures: a clear and valuable account of the poet, his vision and technique.

3. Oligarchy and democracy

Ehrenberg, V., *The Greek State*, Blackwell, 1960. A comprehensive introduction.

Ferguson, J. and Chisholm, K. (ed.), *Political and Social Life in the Great Age of Athens*, Ward Lock, 1978. A useful collection of original material in translation with notes.

Forrest, W.G., *The Emergence of Greek Democracy*, Weidenfeld and Nicholson, 1966. Beautifully illustrated modern history.

Joint Association of Classical Teachers, *The World of Athens: An Introduction to Classical Athenian Culture*, CUP 1984. A similar collection.

Jones, A.H.M., *Athenian Democracy*, Blackwell, 1957. A solidly reliable account of its subject.

Myres, J.L., *The Political Ideas of the Greeks*, Arnold, 1927. A still useful introduction by a scholar of great learning.

Zimmern, Sir Alfred, *The Greek Commonwealth*, Clarendon Press, 1931. A brilliant, though somewhat idealistic book mainly on Periclean Athens. Some think it old-fashioned; it is still good, especially on values.

4. Philosophical ethics

The most thorough account in English of Greek philosophy to Aristotle is

Guthrie, W.K.C., *A History of Greek Philosophy* 6 vols, CUP, 1962-81.

The most useful single-volume is perhaps

Copleston, F.C., *A History of Philosophy* 1, Burns, Oates and Washbourne, 1944.

Two summary books on Greek ethics:
Huby, Pamela, *Greek Ethics*, Macmillan, 1967.
Rowe, C., *An Introduction to Greek Ethics*, Hutchinson, 1976.

For the Preplatonics
Kirk, G.S. and Raven, J.E. (rev. M. Schofield), *The Presocratic Philosophers*, CUP, 1983. This gives a selection of passages in Greek with translation and commentaries.

For the Sophists
Guthrie, W.K.C., *The Sophists*, CUP, 1971.
Kerferd, G.B., *The Sophistic Movement*, CUP, 1981.
Untersteiner, M., *The Sophists*. Eng. tr. Blackwell, 1954.

For Socrates
The literature is immense. See
Ferguson, J., *Socrates: A Source-Book*, Macmillan, 1970, which gives the sources in English (in sometimes old versions but some unobtainable elsewhere) with a summary introduction.
Gulley, N., *The Philosophy of Socrates*, Macmillan, 1968. The one useful single-volume treatment, from one single mind.
Guthrie, W.K.C., *Socrates*, CUP, 1971.
Vlastos, G. (ed.), *The Philosophy of Socrates*, Doubleday, 1971. A useful collection of articles.

For Plato
The literature is immense. See
Crombie, I.M., *An Examination of Plato's Doctrines* 2 vols., Routledge and Kegan Paul, 1962-3. By contrast uneven, brilliant and contentious: the first volume deals with man and society.
Gould, J.P.A., *The Development of Plato's Ethics*, CUP, 1955. The most useful one-volume post-war treatment.
Grube, G.M.A., *Plato's Thought*, Methuen, 1935. A convenient one-volume treatment, unoriginal but sound, arranged by topics.
Lodge, R.C., *Plato's Theory of Ethics*, Routledge and Kegan Paul, 1928. A large and rather dull book, which never really caught on, but thorough and useful for reference.
Vlastos, G. (ed.), *Plato* II, Doubleday, 1972. A valuable collection of articles.

For Aristotle
The literature is immense. See
Ackrill, J.L., *Aristotle's Ethics*, Faber and Faber, 1973. A selection of texts in translation with introduction and notes.
Allan, D.J., *The Philosophy of Aristotle*, OUP, 1952. A really masterly brief introduction to the whole philosophy.
Barnes, J. and others (ed.), *Articles on Aristotle* 2: *Ethics and Politics*, Duckworth, 1977. A useful collection.
Hardie, W.F.R., *Aristotle's Ethical Theory*, Clarendon Press, 1968. A critical account organized by topics.

I have drawn on what I wrote in
Ferguson, J., *Aristotle* (TWAS 211), New York: Twayne, 1972.

5. The Hellenistic age

Ferguson, J., *The Heritage of Hellenism*, Thames and Hudson, 1973. A study of the main themes of the period. For Utopias see
Ferguson, J., *Utopias of the Ancient World.*, Thames and Hudson, 1975. This ran into some criticism for its linking of theory and practice (on which the evidence seems to me clear), but is the only convenient conspectus.
Long, A.A., *Hellenistic Philosophy*, Duckworth, 1974.
Long, A.A., and Sedley, D.N., *The Hellenistic Philosophers* 1, CUP, 1987. The latter a source-book in translation with extensive commentary.
Tarn, W.W. and Griffith, G.T., *Hellenistic Civilization*, Arnold, 1952. A seminal book, most attractive and exciting.

For the Cynics see
Dudley, D.R., *A History of Cynicism*, Methuen, 1937.

For the Epicureans
Rist, J.M., *Epicurus: An Introduction*, CUP, 1972.

For the Stoics
Sandbach, F.H., *The Stoics*, Chatto and Windus, 1975, repr. Bristol Classical Press, 1989.

For the Mystery-Religions

Angus, S., *The Mystery-Religions and Christianity*, New York: Scribner, 1925, is still useful. See also

Reitzenstein, R., *Hellenistic Mystery Religions*. Eng. tr. Pittsburgh: Pickwick Press, 1978. A classic and original treatment.

Ancient Sources Quoted

(Those whose work is available in Greek in Diels-Kranz *Fragmente der Vorsokratiker* are marked DK.)

Aelian	(c. AD 170-235) Greek rhetorician at Rome, who was interested in animal anecdotes.
Aelius Aristides	(AD 117 or 129-c. 181) Stylistic orator, something of a hypochondriac.
Aeschines	(c. 397-322 BC) Athenian orator and politician.
Aeschylus	(525-456 BC) Athenian tragic dramatist.
Alcaeus	(early 6th cent. BC) Lyric poet from Lesbos: the poems survive in fragments only.
Alcman	(late 7th cent. BC) Lyric poet from Sparta.
Ambrose	(c. AD 339-397) Christian bishop of Milan.
Antiphon	(5th cent. BC) We know of a rightwing orator and politician of the name (c. 480-411 BC), and also a sophist, almost certainly different. (DK)
Archelaus	(5th cent. BC) Athenian philosopher who may have influenced Socrates. (DK)
Archilochus	(probably 7th cent. BC) Iambic and elegiac poet from island of Paros, strongly personal and original.
Aristophanes	(c. 450-385 BC) Athenian comic dramatist with brilliant dramatic and verse technique and strongly social and political satire.
Aristotle	(384-322 BC) Philosopher and biological scientist from Stagira in N. Greece. He studied with Plato in Athens, and later set up his own 'school'.
Athenaeus	(c. AD 200) Omnivorous reader who wrote a gloriously miscellaneous work *The Professors at Dinner*. He came from Naucratis in Egypt.
Callicles	(late 5th cent. BC) Appears as a character in Plato, *Gorgias* as an ambitious and ruthless

	politician. It is not clear whether he is fact or fiction.
Callinus	(early 7th cent. BC) Elegiac poet from Ephesus.
Cicero	(106-43 BC) Roman orator, statesman and philosopher.
Cleanthes	(331-232 BC) Successor of Zeno as head of the Stoics, a man of religious genius.
Corpus Hermeticum	Collection of (probably) originally twenty philosophical-religious tracts, written in Egypt from the end of the 2nd cent. AD to the end of the third and attributed to Hermes Trismegistus ('Thrice-greatest').
Crates	(c. 365-285 BC) Philosopher, follower of Heraclitus, teaching that the material world is in a state of flux. (DK)
Critias	(c. 460-403 BC) Athenian right-wing politician, one of the 'Thirty Tyrants' after the war with Sparta; also a creative writer and rationalistic thinker. (DK)
Democritus	(c. 460-360 BC) Philosopher from Abdera in Thrace who argued for the atomic structure of the universe. (DK)
Demosthenes	(384-322 BC) Leading Athenian political orator.
Diogenes 'the Dog'	(c. 400-325 BC) Founder of the Cynics, born in Sinope on the Black Sea, exiled; abjured possessions and citizenship in mainland Greece.
Diogenes Laertius	(early 3rd cent. AD) Author of useful but uncritical collection of sketches of the great philosophers.
Empedocles	(c. 493-433 BC) Religious, philosophical and medical thinker from Acragas in Sicily. (DK)
Epictetus	(c. AD 55-135) Former slave who became a leading Stoic philosopher.
Epicurus	(341-270 BC) Athenian, founder of Epicureans, with an atomic theory in physics, and, ethically, the pursuit of 'pleasure' conceived in terms of freedom from disturbance (*ataraxia*), the renunciation of ambition and other desire, and the abolition of fear through scientific understanding.

Euhemerus
(c. 300 BC) Author of a Utopian novel, which incorporated the view that the gods were originally human beings.

Euripides
(c. 485-406 BC) Athenian tragic dramatist, known for his clarity of language, innovation, and the exploration of ideas.

Gorgias
(c. 483-376 BC) Sophist and teacher of rhetoric from Leontini in Sicily. (DK)

Greek Anthology
A collection of some 3700 epigrams from many periods put together in the late 10th cent. AD.

Heraclitus
(c. 500 BC) Philosopher from Ephesus who regarded the world as a flux of opposites held together by a principle of balance. (DK)

Herodotus
(5th cent. BC) The first major historian, a man of restless and insatiable curiosity and rich sympathy, who came from Halicarnassus in Asia Minor.

Hesiod
(c. 700 BC) One of the oldest Greek poets, a farmer from Boeotia, author of the theoretical *Theogony* and the practical *Works and Days*.

Hippocrates
(late 5th cent. BC) Physician from Cos, founder of clinical medicine.

Homer
(c. 700 BC) By tradition a blind bard from Asia Minor or one of the islands. *The Iliad*, an episode from the Trojan War, brings together traditional episodes into an artistic whole. *The Odyssey*, similarly unified, was attributed to the same poet, but is very different in temper. *The Hymns* attributed to him are certainly later compositions.

Iambulus
(c. 250 BC) Author of a romance which incorporated a Utopia.

Isocrates
(436-338 BC) Athenian writer of speeches and treatises, and educationalist.

Lucian
(2nd cent. AD) Satirist from Syria, a witty and skilful writer.

Maximus of Tyre
(c. AD 125-185) Travelling lecturer of persuasive eloquence, who lectured in Rome.

Menander
(c. 341-290 BC) The greatest writer of 'New' Comedy, with lifelike characters, skilfully

	organized plots, and memorable epigrams.
Origen	(c. AD 185-255) Christian thinker and teacher from Alexandria, textual critic, exegete, theologian, and defender of the Christian faith.
Parmenides	(early 5th cent. BC) Philosophical poet from Elea who held that change is logically impossible and all that can be said is 'Being is'. (DK)
Paul	(1st cent. AD) Jew from Tarsus, converted to Christianity, of which he became a leading missionary preacher and exponent in writing.
Phocylides	(6th cent. BC) Aphoristic elegiac and hexameter poet from Miletus.
Pindar	(518-438 BC) Greatest writer of choral lyric poetry, from Boeotia.
Plato	(427-347 BC) Athenian, associate of Socrates, constructor of a great metaphysical system, according to which the material world is unreal, and reality consists in unchanging Forms known only to the mind.
Plutarch	(c. AD 48-122) Writer of essays on moral philosophy, religion and other topics, and of biographies.
Porphyry	(c. AD 232-305) Neoplatonic philosopher and literary scholar.
Protagoras	(5th cent. BC) Greatest of the sophists, humanist and agnostic. (DK)
Pythagoras	(late 6th cent. BC) Politician, mathematician, philosopher and religious thinker, who emigrated from Samos to Croton in S. Italy. (DK)
Sappho	(early 6th cent. BC) One of the greatest women poets of all time, from Lesbos. Her lyrics survive only in tantalizing fragments.
Seneca	(c. 4 BC-AD 65) Roman statesman, philosopher, and man of letters, from Cordoba in Spain. His philosophical 'letters' to Lucilius show a gentle and eclectic Stoicism.
Sibylline Oracles	A collection of hexameter verses, dating perhaps from 2nd. cent. BC to 3rd cent. AD, showing strong Jewish and Christian influence,

	purporting to be prophecies of the pagan Sibyl.
Socrates	(469-399 BC) Leading Athenian thinker and stimulator of though in others, deeply concerned with the *psyche*. Plato was one of his associates.
Solon	(early 6th cent. BC) Athenian statesman and reformer, of moderate views, who wrote in verse about political and ethical issues.
Sophocles	(496-406 BC) Athenian tragic dramatist, a master of plot construction and of dramatic irony.
Stobaeus	(5th cent. AD) John of Stobi, anthologist.
Teles	(3rd cent. BC) Cynic philosopher, author of 'diatribes' or short sermons.
Theognis	(6th cent. BC) Elegiac poet from Megara, whose work has suffered many accretions.
Thrasymachus	(late 5th cent. BC) Sophist from Chalcedon, important for his contributions to rhetorical theory. Plato depicts him maintaining that 'justice' is the interest of the stronger. (DK)
Thucydides	(c. 460-400 BC) Athenian historian of the war between Athens and Sparta.
Tyrtaeus	(7th cent. BC) Elegiac poet from Sparta.
Xenophanes	(6th cent. BC) Poet and philosopher, exiled from Colophon to Sicily, who believed in one ultimate Being, but denied the existence of gods in human form. (DK)
Zeno	(335-263 BC) Founder of Stoics, from Citium in Cyprus, pantheist, with an exalted idea of moral virtue.
Zenodotus	(date unknown) Otherwise unknown epigrammatist.

Glossary of Technical Terms

(transliterated from the Greek unless otherwise indicated)

adikos unjust
agape (Christian) love, seeking another's wellbeing regardless of merit or response
agathos socially effective, 'good'
aidos a sense of shame
aisa a person's lot, Fate
aischros shameful, ugly
akrasia failure in self-control, weakness of will
andreia manliness, courage
aporia helplessness
arete social effectiveness, excellence, (later) virtue
askesis training, discipline
ataraxia freedom from disturbance
barbaroi non-Greeks, 'barbarians'
chrestos useful, good
damos (Linear B) whole people
deilos living in fear
demos common people
dikaios following the norm of society, 'just'
dikaiosyne obedience to the norm of society, 'justice'
dike way of civilised society, custom, 'justice'
dysnomia state of being under bad laws (cf. *nomos*)
eirene peace
elenches liable to reproach
eleutheria freedom of action, freedom
enaisimos accepting one's lot (cf. *aisa*)
eros love, passion
esthlos good
eudaimonia happiness, blessedness, success
eunomia, eunomie state of being under good laws (cf. *nomos*)
eusebeia piety

eusebes pious
fortitudo (Lat. courage) = *andreia*
homonoia unity of outlook or purpose
isos equal
isonomia equality under the law
iustitia (Lat.) obedience to law, 'justice' = *dikaiosyne*
hybris combination of arrogant attitude and violent action
kakos lacking social effectiveness, without excellence, (later) immoral, 'bad'
kakotes absence of social effectiveness or excellence, (later), immorality
kalos excellent, noble, beautiful
ker fate or death
megalopsychia greatness of *psyche*
moira a person's lot, Fate
moros lot, fate
nemesis distribution of that which is due, retribution
nomos the way a thing is apportioned, something practised as right, law, convention
oikos household, family unit
parrhesia freedom of speech
peitho persuasion
philia social tie usually reciprocated, 'friendship'
philos one's own, 'dear', object of natural affection
philotes see *philia*
phronesis good sense
physis the way a thing grows, nature, sometimes reality
polis city-state
ponos labour, toil, hardship
poros ingenuity
prometheia forethought
prudentia (Lat.) good sense = *phronesis*
psyche inner being of a person, moral personality, life, 'soul'
saophron see *sophron*
sapientia (Lat.) wisdom = *sophia*
sophia wisdom
sophron (*saophron*) with a safe or sound mind, moderate
sophrosyne self-discipline, moderation
stasis civil disturbance
synesis sagacity

telos end, goal
temperantia (Lat.) moderation = *sophrosyne*
themis that which is laid down (e.g. a rule)
time honour
tsedeq (Hebr.) righteousness
tyche fortune
virtus (Lat.) manliness, toughness, (later) virtue
wanax (Linear B) overlord
xe(i)nos host, guest, stranger, friend